IMAGES
of America

BUILDING
CHICAGO'S SUBWAYS

This illustration, titled *Hero of Chicago's Subway*, appears in an August 1941 ad for Cutler-Hammer Motor Control in *Fortune* magazine. The "hero" was the company's air pressure switch product, used during mining operations to prevent tunnels from collapsing. But the thousands of workers who dug the subways are the true heroes. As Virgil E. Gunlock, commissioner of the Chicago Department of Subways and Superhighways, noted at the 1951 opening of the Dearborn-Milwaukee Subway, most of the work was done by hand instead of machine due to the close quarters involved. The photograph shows workers engaged in bench mining, digging Chicago's soft blue clay using long knives. (Author's collection.)

ON THE COVER: On January 10, 1939, Chicago's long-held dream of a subway was fast becoming a reality, as workers drilled a preliminary tunnel towards the main route of the State Street Subway. Just 250 feet away from their goal, both machinery and material are being fed into this tunnel to be used for excavating clay removed during tunneling. A car loaded with clay gets pushed along narrow-gauge tracks as thousands of workers are busy building Chicago's first subway. (Author's collection.)

IMAGES
of America

BUILDING
CHICAGO'S SUBWAYS

David Sadowski

ARCADIA
PUBLISHING

Published by Arcadia Publishing
Charleston, South Carolina

Printed in the United States of America

Library of Congress Control Number: 2018930630

For all general information, please contact Arcadia Publishing:
Telephone 843-853-2070
Fax 843-853-0044
E-mail sales@arcadiapublishing.com
For customer service and orders:
Toll-Free 1-888-313-2665

Visit us on the Internet at www.arcadiapublishing.com

Dedicated to the memory of Charles W. Petzold (1930–1994),
chief transportation engineer for the Chicago Department
of Public Works, who worked on projects that extended
the subways. Everyone knew him as "Charlie."

CONTENTS

ACKNOWLEDGMENTS

The author wishes to thank the following individuals, without whose assistance this book would not have been possible: John F. Bromley, Clifford Burnstein, Raymond DeGroote Jr., Gary Kleinedler, Diana L. Koester, Norman Redelsheimer, George Rex, J.J. Sedelmaier, George Trapp, Roman Vovchak, Jeffrey L. Wien, and Kevin Zolkiewicz. Special thanks go to Arcadia Publishing title manager Liz Gurley, who helped make this a much better book.

Useful references for this work include:

Artingstall, William. "Chicago River Tunnels—Their History and Method of Reconstruction." *Journal of the Western Society of Engineers* vol. 16, no. 9 (November 1911): 869–921.
"Chicago Subway." *Architectural Forum* vol. 81, no. 2 (August 1944): 82–86.
The Chicago Subways. Chicago: City of Chicago, 1943.
Congress Rapid Transit. Chicago: Chicago Transit Authority Office of Public Information, 1967.
The Dearborn-Milwaukee-Congress Subway. Chicago: City of Chicago, 1951.
Ickes, Harold L. *The Secret Diary of Harold L. Ickes: Vol. 2, The Inside Struggle, 1936–1939.* New York: Simon & Schuster, 1953.

Unless otherwise noted, all images are from the author's collection.

For further reading, check out the author's transit blog at www.thetrolleydodger.com.

Note: Chicago's street numbering system, in use since the early 1900s, is in the form of a grid, with State Street being the east–west coordinate and Madison Street the north–south. The numbers provided in parentheses after many of the street names will help readers orient themselves to various locations. For example, Western Avenue is 2400 West, which is three miles west of State Street, as there are eight blocks to a mile throughout most of the city.

INTRODUCTION

For millions of Chicagoans, subways are as important as the iconic Loop elevated ("L") as a means of navigating our world-class city. Yet few know the fascinating story behind the subways and how they came to be. Chicago's first subway opened 75 years ago, still within the memory of living Chicagoans. But four decades of wrangling over what to build, where to build it, and how to pay for it divided the city before that.

Over a 20-year period (1938–1958), Chicago built the State Street and Dearborn-Milwaukee Subways, plus a West Side Subway in the middle of the city's first expressway. These were massive construction projects that changed everyday life for all Chicagoans forever. It cost an estimated $75 million to build the first two subways, another $40 million for the Congress rapid transit line, and $183 million for the Congress (now Eisenhower) Expressway—many billions if assessed relative to today's dollar.

THE RIVER TUNNELS

Chicago's first transportation tunnels went under the Chicago River 150 years ago. As the city grew, the volume of boat traffic meant that bridges were often closed, causing a major inconvenience. Tunnels were needed, but private enterprise proved inadequate to the task; therefore, in 1865, the City of Chicago set out to build a river tunnel under Washington Street. Work began, with stops and starts, the following year. The tunnel finally opened on January 1, 1869. This was soon followed by a LaSalle Street tunnel, which opened on July 4, 1871. The timing was fortunate, since the Great Chicago Fire destroyed large parts of the city starting on October 8. Thousands of Chicagoans' lives were saved by escaping through the river tunnels. Wooden bridges burned, and the river boiled.

By the 1880s, the tunnels had fallen into disrepair and were rarely used. Traction companies then leased them from the city and rebuilt them for use by cable cars, which had difficulty crossing bridges. Private enterprise built a third tunnel near Van Buren Street in 1893 for cable cars. Tunnel approaches were steep, with grades of as much as 10 percent.

In 1900, the flow of the Chicago River was reversed to redirect sewage away from Lake Michigan and into the newly constructed Chicago Sanitary and Ship Canal. However, this feat of engineering had unforeseen consequences: it drastically increased the current and exposed the tops of the river tunnels. Now faced with a navigational hazard, city authorities and investors were forced to choose between rebuilding the tunnels out of harm's way or removing them altogether. In 1906, a compromise was reached when the city permitted traction companies to stop using cable cars and rebuild the tunnels for electric streetcar use.

All three tunnels were lowered by 1912. The preferred method was to dig existing tunnels deeper, then lower their roofs. But the LaSalle tunnel flooded while under construction, making this impossible. Once the old tunnel was removed, and a deeper trench dug, a new method was devised. Two steel tubes were fabricated and floated to the work site. Concrete was poured on the steel, and cables held the barge in position as the tubes were sunk into the trench. Then, coffer dams were built at the ends of the tunnel, connected to the approaches, and sealed. This same method was used in 1939 for the State Street Subway.

These new river tunnels (between 1,500 and 2,000 feet long, including approaches) were built so that they could be converted into streetcar subways, but this never happened. In 1939, the LaSalle tunnel was cut off by subway construction, as the new Clark and Lake subway station intersected its south ramp. The other two streetcar tunnels closed in the 1950s. All three tunnels remain intact today, although their approaches have been truncated and filled in.

The Freight Tunnels

In 1899, Chicago granted a private operator the right to build underground tunnels to house telephone wires. By 1906, this firm, eventually called the Chicago Tunnel Company (CTC), had changed its purpose to hauling freight and mail. At its peak, there were 60 miles of CTC tunnels under the city center that connected to the subbasements of many Loop buildings. Never very profitable, the freight tunnels nonetheless demonstrated the feasibility of digging subways through Chicago's soft, watery blue clay.

Chicago's first two subway lines were built at the same level as the freight tunnels, which were used to remove excavated materials. While some of the freight tunnels were cut off and about 2,000 feet were relocated, the freight tunnels remained viable into the 1950s. By then, their main business, hauling heating coal and ashes, had largely disappeared as furnaces were converted to burn oil, and CTC went out of business in 1959. Today, the tunnels are owned by the city and are used for utility cables. They remain heavily guarded and sealed, since an accidental tunnel breach flooded the system in 1992, causing an estimated $1.95 billion in damage.

Make No Little Plans

City planner Daniel Burnham (1846–1912) has been quoted saying, "Make no little plans; they have no magic to stir men's blood and probably themselves will not be realized. Make big plans; aim high in hope and work, remembering that a noble, logical diagram once recorded will never die, but long after we are gone be a living thing, asserting itself with ever growing insistency." These words, a perfect expression of his philosophy, have been a guiding light to Chicago-area planners for over a century.

While the pioneering *Plan of Chicago* (1909) by Burnham and Edward H. Bennett (1874–1954) says little about subways, there were many other planners who took up the cudgel. Chicago's system of elevated trains had hardly been connected via the Loop "L" when there were calls for its removal (as unsightly) and replacement by subways. This intensified when New York City opened the first of its subways in 1904. Due to cost, it was assumed from the beginning that only major cities could afford to build subways, even though in most cases, they were operated by privately owned transit companies.

Mayor Carter H. Harrison Jr. (1860–1953) appointed a Chicago Subway Commission in 1911, and it would continue to work for more than a quarter century. Both rapid transit and streetcar subways were envisioned. By then, the Loop "L" was overcrowded, especially from the north and south. The proposed subway on State Street offered additional capacity. Plans for a second subway, on either Clark Street or Dearborn Street, originated in the 1920s. This line would connect to the existing Logan Square–Humboldt Park "L" via either a subway or elevated tracks along Milwaukee Avenue, a more direct and time-saving path.

Money to build a subway accumulated in a Traction Fund, representing most of the city's share of the net earnings from Chicago's streetcar system. While funds were available for a subway, there was considerable disagreement about how to proceed. There were two schools of thought. One group wanted subways built all over the city to replace all the "L's." The other argued for subways only in the downtown area, due to both their cost and the Loop's density.

By 1915, the Traction Fund held $14 million, but the city had borrowed against it, substituting tax anticipation warrants. Mayor Anton J. Cermak's (1873–1933) administration borrowed against the fund again during the Great Depression. Some thought State Street merchants should pay for the subway, since it would make their properties more valuable. When construction nearly began in 1931, the city wanted merchants to pay 60 percent of the cost. As economic conditions worsened and a legal battle developed over taxing Loop merchants, subway plans were put on hold. By then, over $4 million had been spent on planning.

After Cermak was assassinated in 1933 by Giuseppe Zangara, who may or may not have been aiming at president-elect Franklin D. Roosevelt (FDR), he was succeeded by Edward J. Kelly

(1876–1950). In 1938, Kelly applied for federal aid to build the State Street Subway and two downtown streetcar subways. FDR's administration had money available for large-scale projects through the Public Works Administration (PWA), headed by Secretary of the Interior Harold L. Ickes. The PWA was willing to pay for 45 percent, working in partnership with local governments on projects that were "shovel-ready," in an effort to put people back to work in useful jobs, if work could be completed in 18 months.

Ickes was a liberal Republican and progressive "good government" reformer who had been active in Chicago politics for 40 years. He was an enemy of Samuel Insull (1859–1938), who controlled the Chicago Rapid Transit Company until his utility empire collapsed in 1932. Ickes was also a rival of Mayor Kelly and considered running against him. Ickes felt the people of Chicago deserved a subway, but since he had serious reservations about Kelly's plans, he appointed a blue-ribbon commission to study and amend the proposal in just two months' time.

The committee, including such luminaries as engineers Robert Ridgway (1862–1938) and Joshua D'Esposito (1878–1954), approved the State Street Subway but rejected streetcar subways. The commission preferred a second subway via Milwaukee Avenue and Dearborn Street. While streetcar subways would reduce congestion on downtown surface streets, it was felt the Milwaukee-Dearborn Subway would do better, as it would inevitably shift riders from the surface to the rapid transit system.

Dearborn Street was only one block from State Street, an easy transfer. Additional recommended changes were cherry-picked from local plans that had been around for years. Ickes accepted the changes and offered the city a grant on a "take it or leave it" basis and added stipulations requiring that the city unify the three major local transit operators, commit to future subway extensions, and build a west side superhighway along Congress Street. Kelly and the city council accepted this plan on October 28, 1938. Less than two months later, ground was broken for the city's first-ever subway. Construction on the Milwaukee-Dearborn Subway began a few months later. It would take over 20 years to fulfill this plan.

THE INITIAL SYSTEM OF SUBWAYS

The city moved quickly to build its first two subways, putting 7,000 people to work. The two tubes for Phase 1 were nearly complete by the end of 1941. By then, America was at war. Construction materials were prioritized for defense and were harder to obtain. Work stopped on the 80 percent–complete Dearborn-Milwaukee Subway in 1942 as there were not enough steel cars on hand to operate it. Many Chicagoans were engaged in war work, and gasoline and tires were rationed, so the State Street Subway received a priority, since many workers were dependent on public transportation. It was finished and opened to the public on October 17, 1943. Work on the second subway resumed after the war ended in 1945.

By this time, the Illinois legislature had created the Chicago Transit Authority (CTA), which took over the surface and rapid transit systems in 1947. After new railcars were purchased, the CTA's Dearborn-Milwaukee Subway opened on February 25, 1951. This was extended west to connect with the new West Side Subway (also known as the Congress Expressway median line) on June 22, 1958. Now Chicago had nearly 10 miles of subways with 18 stations.

SUBWAYS AND SUPERHIGHWAYS

Construction of Chicago's west side expressway displaced an estimated 13,000 people and 400 businesses between 1949 and 1961. Many politicians thought they were eliminating blighted areas while at the same time building a highway and relocating a rapid transit line to serve the public. Efforts were made to assist with relocation, but many people were simply left to fend for themselves. The city thought the west side was in an economic decline, and the new highway would revitalize it. The west side turnaround took decades, and there were further dislocations, as Little Italy was largely destroyed in the 1960s to build the University of Illinois's Chicago campus. But now the expressway, campus, and the adjacent medical center complex form an anchor, creating expanding economic growth in the area.

The five-year (1953–1958) construction of the expressway through Chicago's west side meant relocating part of the Garfield Park "L" that was in its path into a temporary right-of-way in the south half of Van Buren Street. The Chicago, Aurora & Elgin Railway (CA&E) operated electric interurban trains to downtown Chicago over the Garfield Park "L" to the Wells Street Terminal. CA&E refused to operate trains in a city street without grade crossings and cut back service to Forest Park. Loss of a one-seat ride and the slow temporary service caused the CA&E to abandon passenger service suddenly in the middle of the day on July 3, 1957, stranding thousands of commuters. Efforts to save the railroad were futile, and it was dismantled starting in 1961. Most of its right-of-way is now the Illinois Prairie Path, the first "rails to trails" project in the country.

The city's plans to relocate the Garfield Park "L" changed over time, from partial to complete replacement. After five years of difficult construction, the new median line opened as far as Cicero Avenue on June 22, 1958, even as work continued in suburban Oak Park and Forest Park. The Congress Rapid Transit line was finished in 1961, with the opening of permanent stations west of Cicero Avenue. By then, the Northwest and South Expressways (since renamed for John F. Kennedy and Daniel Ryan) were largely built, with medians set aside for future transit use. Federal mass transit funding finally became available in the mid-1960s. Mayor Richard J. Daley was an important ally of Pres. Lyndon B. Johnson and obtained funding for rapid transit extensions along these two expressways. Ultimately, the project to extend service on Chicago's northwest side included a mile-long subway under Milwaukee and Kimball Avenues, which opened in 1970 with two new stations. This line was further extended to O'Hare Airport in 1984, with a short subway in the terminal area.

Chicago's latest subway, a 4,400-foot tunnel connecting the Howard and Dan Ryan lines, opened in 1993 but includes no stations. Chicago's newest rapid transit, the 1993 Orange Line, is all elevated, as is most of the Pink Line, a 2006 realignment of the Douglas Park "L" following the same 1954–1958 route used during expressway construction.

While subways were once intended to replace Chicago's "L", they are expensive and only built when necessary. Subways coexist with the iconic elevated Loop, and the "L" is here to stay, but Chicago's subways do the heavy lifting in our rapid transit system today.

One

THE RIVER TUNNELS

This remarkable c. 1870s photograph shows the east entrance to the Washington Street tunnel prior to 1884, when it was rebuilt for cable car use. Within 10 years of its 1869 opening, the tunnel was not used much, especially in the winter, as there were water leaks and it often filled up with ice. (Photograph by John Carbutt.)

1106. Chicago River Tunnell, Chicago, Ill.

To commemorate the opening of the Washington Street river tunnel, Chicago's first, *Harper's Weekly* ran this illustration on January 20, 1869, offering a comprehensive view. The horse-drawn streetcars of the time, introduced a decade earlier, did not need to use the tunnel, as they could easily traverse bridges. This tunnel was 1,605 feet long, including approaches, and cost $517,000 for the city to build.

This illustration from the May 11, 1867, issue of *Harper's Weekly* shows the Washington Street tunnel under construction. The first such man-made tunnel under a river opened in 1843 in London, under the River Thames. It pioneered the shield method of tunnel boring and helped inspire the Chicago River tunnels.

The *Harper's Weekly* issue released on May 24, 1890, shows the LaSalle Street river tunnel as rebuilt for cable car use. Construction started on November 3, 1869, and the tunnel originally opened on July 4, 1871. It was 1,890 feet long and cost the city $566,000. The two river tunnels helped save thousands of lives during the Great Chicago Fire on October 8, 1871, as they were a means of escape after wooden bridges burned and the river boiled.

Another view, looking south, is shown in this image of the LaSalle Street tunnel, published in the May 3, 1890, *Harper's Weekly*. Cable cars are generally associated with hilly San Francisco and not flat Chicago, but at its peak, Chicago had the most extensive cable car system in the country, with 41 miles of routes. The last Chicago cable car ran on October 21, 1906, when electric streetcar technology replaced it.

Cable cars are shown using the LaSalle Street tunnel under the Chicago River some time before 1906. A continuously moving cable ran through a trough between the rails; a "grip" cable car would grab onto it and be pulled along. This first car would often, in turn, pull trailers. Cable cars did well in Chicago despite the cold, snowy winters. The view in this photograph, likely from the late 1890s, looks north where the "L" is already present on Lake Street.

By May 13, 1912, the LaSalle Street tunnel was completely rebuilt. All three tunnels were lowered between 1906 and 1912, as their tops had been exposed once the Chicago River current was reversed in 1900. The tunnel collapsed while being rebuilt, so a new strategy was devised. Steel tubes were fabricated, had concrete added, and were floated into position, where they were sunk into a trough. Coffer dams were built on the north and south ends of the tubes and connected to the approaches. This same method was used in 1939 for the State Street Subway. Subway construction closed the LaSalle tunnel in 1939, as its south approach was cut off by what is now the Clark and Lake station on today's CTA Blue Line. (Photograph by William M. Christie.)

By June 29, 1953, when Robert Selle took this picture, the LaSalle Street streetcar tunnel had been closed for more than 13 years. This view looks south from Hubbard Street. The ramp in the background, at Kinzie Street, leads down to North Water Street and was built in 1928, when a bridge was built over the Chicago River at LaSalle Street. Since the streetcar tunnel entrance was filled in, many have since misidentified this as the streetcar tunnel entrance. The tunnel itself still exists.

Two streetcars, Chicago Surface Lines trolleys 561 and 1466, meet at the entrance to the Van Buren streetcar tunnel in the 1940s. Car 1466 is signed as a demonstrator for training purposes. Due to the steep grade in this tunnel, it was not used in regular service after 1924. This tunnel was out of service for one year (1915–1916) due to the construction of Union Station nearby. (Photograph by Joe L. Diaz.)

Chicago Transit Authority streetcar 475 emerges from the east end of the Washington Street tunnel at Franklin Street. Once the various streetcar lines that had used it were replaced by buses, the Washington Street tube, the last of the three streetcar tunnels, was closed in 1954. (Photograph by Robert Selle, Wien-Criss Archive.)

On November 6, 1941, seven people were injured and 100 were shaken up after two streetcars crashed in the Washington Street tunnel. As one car went uphill, its brakes failed. It rolled backwards and ran into the front of the streetcar following behind it. (ACME Photograph.)

Two

THE FREIGHT TUNNELS

Between 1906 and 1959, the CTC and its predecessors operated a fleet of electric narrow-gauge locomotives that hauled practically everything except passengers through an extensive system of tunnels 40 feet below the surface of downtown streets. They were completely dug out by hand using large knives. (J.J. Sedelmaier Collection.)

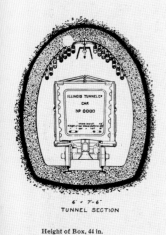

6' × 7'-6"
TUNNEL SECTION

Height of Box, 44 in.
Width of Box, 48 in.

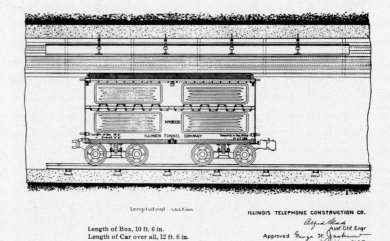

Longitudinal section

Length of Box, 10 ft. 6 in.
Length of Car over all, 12 ft. 6 in.

ILLINOIS TELEPHONE CONSTRUCTION CO.

Asst. Chf. Engr
Approved
Genl. Mgr. & Chf. Engr

Drawing No: ....

This end- and side-view diagram shows the car dimensions and location of trolley wire and telephone cables in the freight tunnels. The tunnels were small enough that they did not need steel reinforcement. All telephone lines were removed from the tunnels by 1920, as the CTC's business model had changed to hauling freight. (J.J. Sedelmaier Collection.)

The freight tunnels gave downtown merchants an alternative to moving their goods through the increasingly crowded streets, cluttered with autos, trucks, streetcars, and pedestrians. They served downtown warehouses like this one.

Until the 1950s, coal was widely used for heating, and most of the Chicago Tunnel Company's business was hauling coal and ashes. Steam locomotives and cars hauled ashes to the lakefront and dumped remnants into Lake Michigan. Waste materials were also used for landfill that added to Chicago's lakefront. Over time, more and more buildings converted their furnaces to oil. After the market for coal collapsed, the CTC went bankrupt, and the freight tunnels were closed in 1959. But almost all are still in place and are now owned by the city.

Above, on February 16, 1915, cars filled with ashes from the Marshall Field's boiler room are ready for transport to the tunnel company's Lake Front Disposal Station. In the c. 1915 photograph below, freight is being loaded onto tunnel cars in the shipping room of the Murdock Company, a large commercial house. The freight cars were then moved to an elevator by the electric motor truck seen in the foreground and brought to the level of the tunnels.

The freight tunnels sought out post office business, but it was not very profitable. This did inspire the creation of the 6.5-mile-long London Post Office Railway (aka "Mail Rail"), which operated from 1927 to 2003. In 2017, a portion of the London tunnel became a museum, unlike the Chicago freight tunnels, which are strictly off-limits to the public. In this picture, US mail, taken from railroad trains and onto tunnel cars, is being delivered to a receiving room at the post office via conveyor belt.

Merchandise rack car 5000 was built by Bettendorf Car Company. When the freight tunnels closed in 1959, a few pieces of equipment and even one locomotive were abandoned in the tunnels.

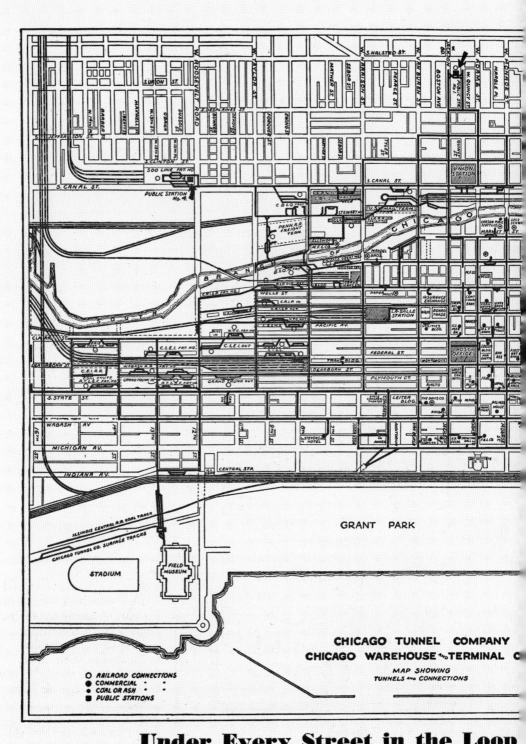

CHICAGO TUNNEL COMPANY
CHICAGO WAREHOUSE AND TERMINAL C

MAP SHOWING
TUNNELS AND CONNECTIONS

O RAILROAD CONNECTIONS
● COMMERCIAL · ·
● COAL OR ASH
■ PUBLIC STATIONS

Under Every Street in the Loop

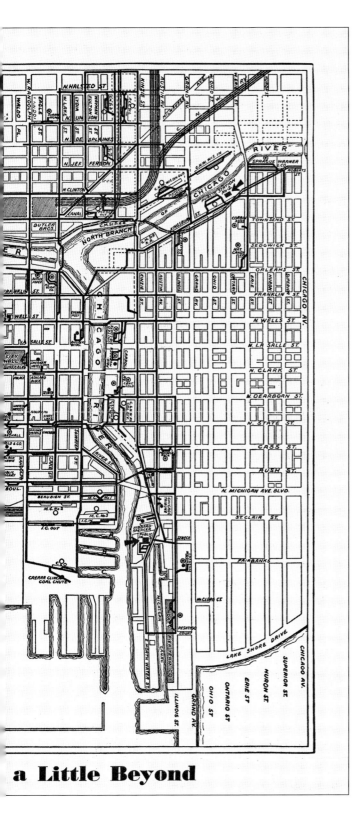

a Little Beyond

This map details the Chicago Tunnel Company's approximately 60-mile downtown system as it existed in November 1938, just prior to the start of subway construction. About 2,000 feet of freight tunnels were relocated due to the subway, while others were simply truncated. Subway construction was made more convenient by the freight tunnels, which were used to haul away excavated clay. (J.J. Sedelmaier Collection.)

Miles and miles of these tunnels still exist under Chicago's downtown, but security was heightened after the tunnels flooded in 1992. They remain a tremendous asset to the city, since they are used by utilities to run fiber optics and other such cables. These photographs show the freight tunnels on November 30, 2017. (Photographs by Roman Vovchak.)

Three

MAKE NO LITTLE PLANS

The "L" was still Chicago's only rapid transit in 1938, as this Chicago Rapid Transit Company (CRT) map declares. The Loop could only handle so much traffic, and there were choke points like the intersection at Lake and Wells Streets, where lines crossed each other. Elsewhere on the system, three lines (Logan Square/Humboldt Park, Garfield Park, and Douglas Park) came together at Marshfield Junction on Chicago's west side. There was a crucial need for more capacity but no chance of building more "L's, which the city hoped eventually to eliminate. Subways were the answer. (J.J. Sedelmaier Collection.)

By the 1920s, some sought a subway under State Street to reduce congestion, while others, such as city planner Edward H. Bennett, thought it would only make the problem worse. As seen in this picture, Chicago's downtown streets were full of cars, trucks, trolleys, and people. The caption of this picture notes that "the problem of getting about in a great modern city . . . actuates the improvement of new streets and new routes in the effort to relieve city congestion." Subways were just such "new streets" that cities felt justified in building to relieve this congestion, despite their cost. Instead of subways, Bennett favored elevated pedestrian walkways.

This 1909 subway plan is one of many unrealized drafts. The idea of an east–west subway for streetcars (and later buses) persisted for another 50 years but never came to fruition. Instead of a four-track subway on Wabash Avenue, two tracks each were eventually built at State Street and Dearborn Street.

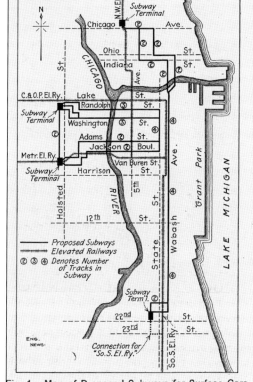

Fig. 1. Map of Proposed Subways for Surface Cars and Elevated Railway Trains in Chicago.

Harold L. Ickes, fourth from left, was involved in Chicago politics as early as 1897. Considered a reformer, he usually found himself on the losing side. Ickes took an interest in transit issues, though, and the "Subway Question" in particular. He is pictured in Philadelphia on October 12, 1931, with other members of the Chicago Subway Commission, comprised of city officials, lawyers, and real estate men, as they arrived at the Broad Street station to study Philadelphia's rapid transit facilities. Philadelphia's Broad Street Subway was relatively new, having opened in stages beginning on September 1, 1928. In 1938, as secretary of the interior and head of the Public Works Administration (PWA), Ickes approved federal funding for Chicago's first subways. (ACME Photograph.)

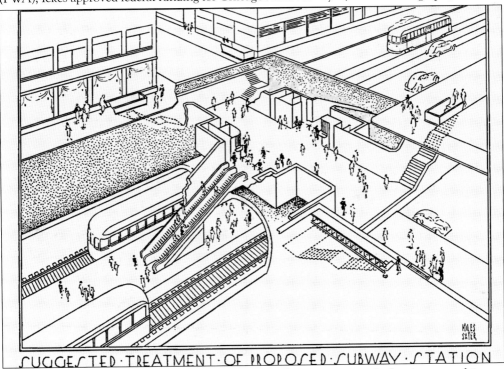

SUGGESTED · TREATMENT · OF · PROPOSED · SUBWAY · STATION

This 1938 drawing shows how the city intended its subway stations to look prior to reaching an agreement with the federal government for a grant to cover 45 percent of the cost. Presidents' Conference Committee (PCC) streetcars, only recently put into service on Madison Street, are running in a subway, with stations built at street intersections. The PWA ultimately rejected streetcar subways but did support a rapid transit subway under Dearborn Street and Milwaukee Avenue. Stations were built mid-block in the Loop to allow for two east-west streetcar subways in the future, which were never built. The Chicago Transit Authority phased out streetcars by 1958.

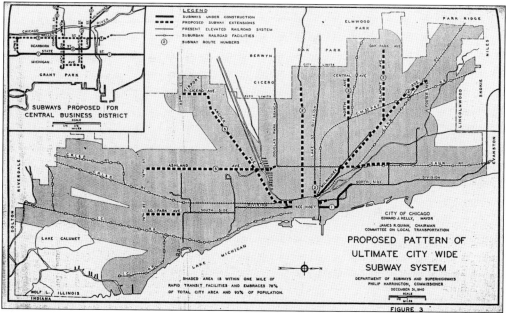

PWA chief Harold Ickes called the State Street Subway "dinky" and pressed the City of Chicago to plan for more subways. This map shows the city's plans for subway extensions in all directions as of December 31, 1940.

In response to city demands that the struggling Chicago Rapid Transit Company replace its aging wooden car fleet, CRT built a mock-up of a proposed 5000-series car, influenced by various experimental New York City subway cars. The four articulated Chicago units, eventually built in 1947–1948, closely resembled the Brooklyn-Manhattan Transit (BMT) "Bluebirds."

By 1941, the city's plans had evolved, with a mezzanine-level station mid-block that would lead to a lower-level subway (to reduce the amount of utility relocation) and new all-steel rapid transit cars that look like the BMT Bluebirds. These were the most advanced rapid transit cars of their time and the first to use PCC technology, which had already revolutionized the streetcar industry.

Between 1939 and 1940, the Clark Equipment Company built six articulated units, referred to as the BMT "Bluebirds." Although the Bluebirds only had a top speed of 40 miles per hour, they had fast acceleration and were intended for use on both subway and elevated lines as "fast locals" that could keep up with older cars used in express service. BMT ordered 50 such units, but once the privately held transit company came under municipal ownership in June 1940, the order was cancelled, and only five units and the prototype were delivered. As oddball equipment, they were mainly used in shuttle operations and were scrapped in 1957. Chicago's first postwar rapid transit cars were largely based on the design of the Bluebirds.

On February 7, 1939, a workman is installing seating on a new BMT Bluebird subway car at the Clark Equipment Company plant in Battle Creek, Michigan. The Bluebirds' improved amenities included more comfortable seats and forced-air ventilation. (Clark Equipment Company.)

Chicago's subway planners wanted new railcars based on the BMT Bluebirds, but no new equipment could be ordered until after the war. Meanwhile, they created this fanciful postcard view of Chicago's new State Street Subway. The rendering, made from a 1943 photograph, features a BMT-style Bluebird rapid transit car in place of the 1920s-era equipment CRT was forced to use.

The cash-strapped CRT could only afford to order four new trainsets when World War II ended. This new CRT articulated "Doodlebug" 5001 was photographed in 1947 at Laramie Yard on the Garfield Park "L" after being put into service. Some aspects of these cars, such as articulation, were experimental and did not pan out, and it was for the best that more were not ordered. By waiting, the CTA made substantial improvements to their design. (Photograph by George Snyder.)

On February 24, 1950, CTA "L" riders were cheerful despite the obvious lack of amenities on the train. Older cars were heated using coal-burning stoves. During a particularly cold winter, the CTA had to cut off all heat in "L" trains to conserve their coal supplies. Fortunately, new rapid transit cars were delivered later the same year, equipped with electric heat.

Subway tunnels had no sprinkler systems or water pipes, and in the case of fire, firemen had to bring hoses down from the surface. On July 23, 1944, a Lake Street "L" train blazed, leaving one car completely gutted. Indicating great concern, the city banned wooden cars and issued a book on the subject, *Fire Protection in Chicago Subways*, under Virgil E. Gunlock's byline in 1951.

The Underground station at Arnos Grove, in the London borough of Enfield, was built in 1932 and influenced the design of the aboveground North and Clybourn station house in Chicago. Designed by famed architect Charles Holden (1875–1960) in the modern style and constructed of concrete and red and blue brick, with steel-framed windows, Arnos Grove has a bright interior with a central supporting column. It is thought this design may have been influenced by the Stockholm City Library (built in 1928 and designed by Erik Gunnar Asplund), which Holden had visited in 1930. This was one of several modern Tube stations designed by Holden in the 1930s. (Photograph by George Rex.)

In 2009, the North and Clybourn station was still largely in "as-built" condition, but it would soon get a face-lift. This station, designed in 1939–1941, is a somewhat scaled-down version of a Charles Holden–type London Underground station, with many of the same styling features. The Chicago firm of Shaw, Naess & Murphy was responsible. Alfred P. Shaw (1895–1970) was probably the main architect of the only aboveground station on the Initial System of Subways. (Photograph by Kevin Zolkiewicz.)

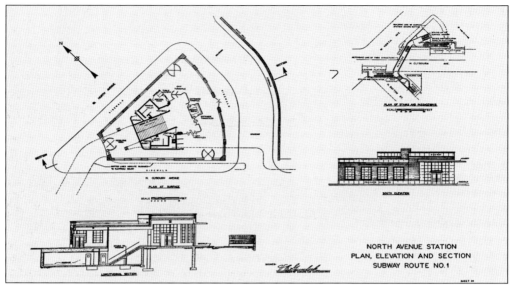

NORTH AVENUE STATION
PLAN, ELEVATION AND SECTION
SUBWAY ROUTE NO.1

The North and Clybourn station was not part of the city's original plans, which called for the State Street Subway to end at Chicago Avenue. The PWA commissioners moved the connection farther north to bypass a triple curve that still slows down "L" trains. This had been suggested locally by subway critics in 1930.

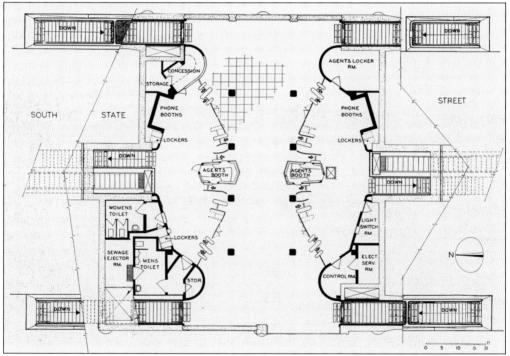

The layout of the mezzanine-level station on the State Street Subway provides space for concessions, pay telephones, public washrooms, and even parcel lockers. The lockers and washrooms were early casualties, and the widespread use of cell phones has made pay phones an endangered species. Access to track level was by means of stairs and escalators (called "moving stairways" on some subway plans).

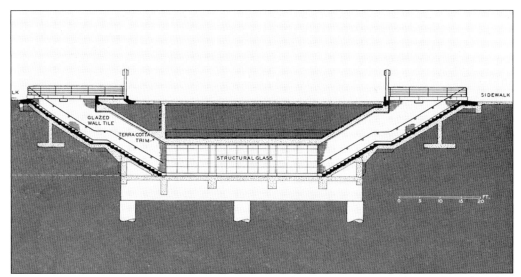

The downtown mezzanine-level subway stations made extensive use of subway tile, referred to here as "structural glass." Chicago was once a center of terra-cotta production, so much so that there is a street called Terra Cotta Place, but unlike a lot of terra-cotta designs, this new type of ceramic was largely devoid of ornamentation.

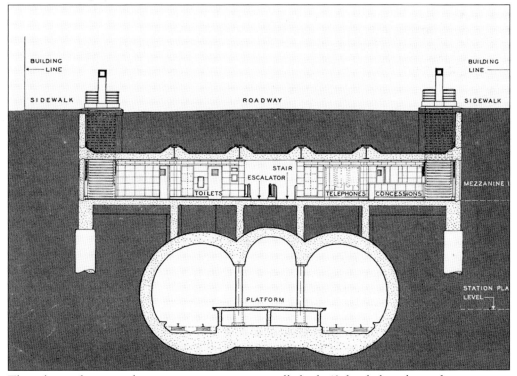

The subway, shown in this cross section, was generally built 43 feet below the surface streets in the downtown area, about the same level as the freight tunnels. A few tunnels were relocated due to subway construction, but nearly six miles of the freight tunnels were simply cut off, as there were so many tunnels in the Loop that alternate routings could be used to service the Chicago Tunnel Company's clients.

AN INTERURBAN ROADWAY IN 1950. PARALLEL TEAMING, TROLLEY AND PLEASURE WAYS.

Daniel Burnham was already hard at work on the famous *Plan of Chicago* with collaborator Edward H. Bennett when this prescient 1908 illustration appeared in one of their side projects: *Inter-Urban Roadways*, published by the Commercial Club of Chicago. Burnham and Bennett, credited with inspiring the Congress Expressway, also predicted railroads in highway median strips by 1950. By then, plans were already well under way to put a rapid transit line in the median of the Congress Expressway. Chicago later built two additional expressway median lines. (Chicago History Museum.)

Chicago embraced expressway medians for transit use but was not the first to do so. From 1940 to 1952, the Pacific Electric (PE) interurban in Los Angeles ran in the median of the Hollywood Freeway through Cahuenga Pass. Unfortunately, the PE system was not appreciated by local officials, and it was abandoned by 1961. Parts of it have since been reactivated. (Courtesy of John F. Bromley.)

Early subway plans called for a four-track downtown subway, but there was no need for both express and local trains in the Loop. As built, the first two subways did add four tracks to downtown capacity, but much of the existing "L" system could hardly be called "express." The "L" and the surface system were competitors, and the CTA was created in part to configure the two systems to work together, using the surface system as a feeder to the faster "L's and subways. Convinced that faster service was the key to increasing ridership, the CTA eliminated lightly used branch lines, closed several stations, and introduced the A/B "skip stop" service advertised in this 1949 brochure.

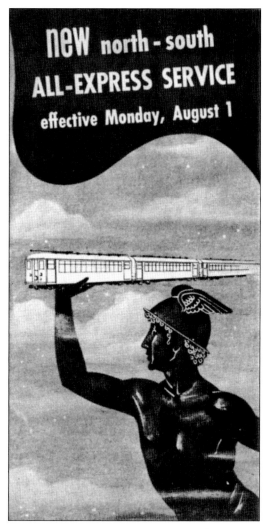

Emboldened by improvements in service, speed, and ridership on the new Dearborn-Milwaukee Subway, the CTA worked in partnership with industry professionals to develop high-speed rapid transit cars, as evidenced by this 1955 test run announcement, where a modified train reached speeds of 75 miles per hour on northside express tracks.

On October 3, 1955, Virgil E. Gunlock (left), CTA chairman; Mayor Daley (center); and Walter J. McCarter, CTA general manager, took part in the speed run on Chicago's northside "L". When plans were announced for a rapid transit line in the middle of an expressway, the public expected such trains to go as fast as autos. The CTA set about developing high-speed motors, which were first used on the 2000-series cars in 1964. Today's railcars can go 70 miles per hour, although they are limited to just 55.

This 1959 CTA illustration shows how the rapid transit extension along the Northwest Expressway (now Kennedy) was originally intended to connect with the existing Logan Square "L". Between Rockwell and Talman Avenues (approximately 2615 West), the existing "L" would have turned north and descended into an open-cut subway before emerging in the expressway median. Neighborhood activists lobbied instead for a subway extension along Milwaukee Avenue to the city limits, asserting that the city had promised the federal government in 1939 that it would build such an extension and was thus obligated. The Milwaukee-Kimball Subway, opened in 1970, was a compromise solution, retaining most of the expressway routing but with two additional stations serving Logan Square. This view looks south.

Four

THE STATE STREET SUBWAY

A crowd, probably full of city employees (note the abundance of pro-Kelly signs), watches the December 17, 1938, ceremonies at State Street and Chicago Avenue marking the start of work on Chicago's first subways. PWA subway commissioner Robert Ridgway (1862–1938) attended the event but suffered a heart attack on his way back to New York City and died two days later. (ACME Photograph.)

Above, Secretary of the Interior Harold L. Ickes (left) speaks at the December 17, 1938, ceremony commemorating commencement of the subway project, while his political rival, Chicago mayor Edward J. Kelly, looks on at right. The event was broadcast on local radio. Later on, Ickes and Kelly were photographed dislodging a cobblestone with a pneumatic shovel, ceremoniously breaking ground on the project. (Above, ACME Photograph; left, City of Chicago.)

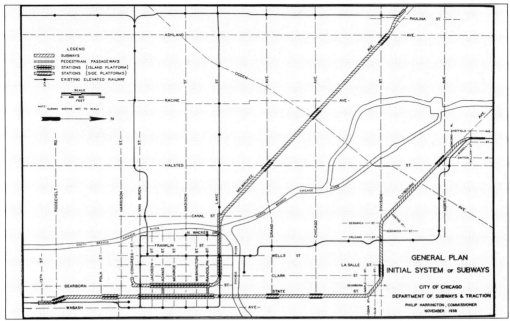

Chicagoans were puzzled in 1938 when the PWA and the city approved plans for a Dearborn-Milwaukee Subway that ended abruptly at Dearborn and Congress Streets. But Phase 1 plans always envisioned future subways. Phase 2, adopted in 1939, extended this subway west along Congress Street, under the Chicago River and the Main Post Office, before surfacing near Halsted Street (800 West). West of there, plans were still being formulated for the Congress Street Superhighway. (City of Chicago.)

This unique composite combines photographs and drawings to show how mining was done in the downtown area. Due to the water content of the underlying clay, tunneling used the shield method, pressurized air, and an air lock. Portions of the freight tunnels were used to remove excavated materials. Tunnels that interfered with the new bore were cut off and filled with cement. The near-south Loop area shown in this picture has drastically changed since 1940 and is now filled with upscale townhouses and condominiums. (Peter Fish Studios for the City of Chicago.)

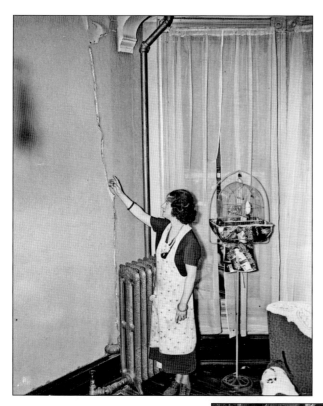

On May 17, 1939, Lillian Edwards examines a crack in the wall of her apartment, which she attributed to nearby subway construction. Workers tried to minimize damage to nearby buildings, but some was inevitable. The city paid property owners for such damages.

Subway excavation in the Loop was literally a mining operation, as shown in this July 21, 1939, view. Crowds of workers, subway officials, and firemen entered a tunnel work site after a fire broke out. Chicago's downtown was originally a swamp, or marsh, that was filled in. Tunneling in the Loop involved use of a shield and compressed air. Mezzanine-level station entrances were located mid-block and were built using the cut-and-cover technique.

While Chicago is not as old as some cities on the East Coast, urban archaeology remnants did pop up from time to time during subway construction. On February 1, 1940, worker Mike Sunta unearthed an underground tube once used by Chicago cable cars. The Chicago cable car system preceded electric streetcars and was used from 1882 to 1906.

On February 13, 1939, Alice Ola (later Harris) (1915–1978) of Cleveland became the first woman to descend into the new Chicago subway. She posed for pictures with Frank J. Herlihy, president of the construction company building this section of tunnel. Ola worked as a stewardess on New York–to–Chicago flights for United Airlines. She was inevitably nicknamed "Alice in Underland" by tunnel workmen. The Chicago subway project got national attention, and some used it for publicity stunts such as this. Construction work was done by several different companies. (ACME Photograph.)

On June 13, 1940, tunnel mining operations are taking place in the State Street contract area S-3 (downtown). By the end of 1941, the tunnels were complete for both subways, but they had no tracks, signals, or finished stations. (City of Chicago.)

In a similar fashion to how the LaSalle Street streetcar tube was laid into the Chicago River in 1911, prefabricated steel tubes for the State Street Subway's river crossing were moved by barge on October 16, 1939. They were moved via the Calumet River on Chicago's far south side into Lake Michigan, then through a lock, and were sunk into position. (ACME Photograph.)

The tunnel where the State Street Subway crosses under the Chicago River is shown on March 24, 1943, and greatly resembles the LaSalle Street streetcar tunnel, which used a very similar method of construction throughout 1911–1912. Every few miles, there are crossover tracks in case trains need to be rerouted around each other via the other track or must be turned back. (ACME Photograph.)

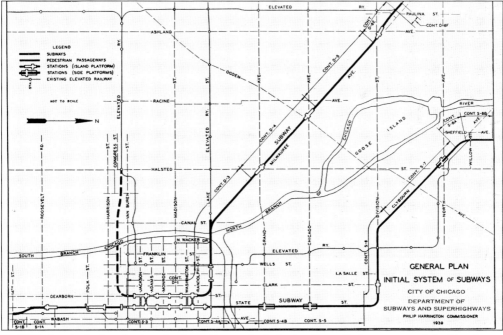

By 1939, the city's plans had evolved, and it now include the Phase 2 plan to extend the Dearborn-Milwaukee Subway west along Congress Street to a new connection with the Garfield Park "L". The Congress Expressway is not yet shown, as those plans were not approved by city council until 1940; however, the locations of various subway contract areas are detailed. (City of Chicago.)

Workmen are putting State Street back together at Monroe Street on August 25, 1941. A mezzanine-level subway station was built here via the cut-and-cover technique. The street is supported by a network of steel beams, forming a virtual bridge. Streetcar tracks have been diverted to the outer edges of the street while new permanent tracks are set in concrete. (J.J. Sedelmaier Collection.)

Building the subway was a dirty business on October 1, 1939, as this muddy scene shows. The area at left, after being filled in with concrete, will become a station platform. By then, nearly one mile of tunnel will be complete. (ACME Photograph.)

In the left image, showing the shape of things to come, models Mrs. Leroy Post (left) and Mrs. C.L. Mann, both of Evanston, pose as would-be subway riders, although no tracks are yet in place. At right, models Valeria Losiniecki (left), 18, and Eva Frendreis, 21, are shown coming up a subway escalator to an unfinished mezzanine station on March 18, 1943. There are bare wires hanging from the ceiling, and the floor area has been heavily retouched. Furs were a popular display of status, especially mink.

This section of subway at the North and Clybourn station was virtually complete except for tracks by January 1, 1942. By then, the nation was at war with the Axis powers (Germany, Italy, and Japan), and materials needed to complete the subway were reserved for the war effort.

In March or April 1943, only the southbound track leading into the north portal of the State Street Subway has been completed. Once the first two stations were finished, at Clark and Division Streets and Jackson Boulevard and State Street, it was possible to use this single track to operate test trains into the subway as a shuttle operation. Mayor Kelly, running for reelection, boosted his prospects by showing people that the subway was at last a reality, even if it was not quite finished. *Life* magazine, no friend of Kelly's, hailed it as a brilliant political move. By the public opening in October, 10,000 rides were given out. (City of Chicago.)

By March 29, 1943, when this picture was taken at the north portal to the State Street Subway, the southbound track and two stations were finished, enough to begin offering test rides to officials and war bond buyers. Veteran CRT motorman Charles R. Blade is at the controls. (ACME Photograph.)

In late 1942, the City of Chicago agreed to let the privately owned Chicago Rapid Transit Company operate the State Street Subway. In March 1943, test runs began in the subway using the one completed track. CRT's newest equipment was about 20 years old, and there were no immediate prospects for obtaining new railcars in wartime. CRT had 455 all-steel rapid transit cars, enough to at least begin service. Ultimately, the subway did not materially affect CRT's precarious financial situation, increasing income and expenses by about the same amount. (City of Chicago.)

In April 1943, just prior to the mayoral election, the City of Chicago held an inspection trip in the still-uncompleted State Street Subway, with only one track in service. Each attendee received a souvenir pin. Some attendees were government officials, while others were prominent citizens, invitees, or purchasers of war bonds.

Mayor Edward J. Kelly (second row, sixth from right) and a large delegation of city and federal officials—including Secretary of the Interior Harold Ickes (second row, second from right)—pose for pictures during the first official subway inspection trip on April 2, 1943. Veteran motorman Charles Rudolph Blade (kneeling at right) piloted the train, shown at Jackson Boulevard and State Street. Blade was born in Sweden in 1891, immigrated to the United States in 1909, and became a naturalized citizen in 1917. He served his country in the Navy during World War I and worked as a rapid transit motorman from 1911 until he retired in 1955. He died in 1983 aged 91. (City of Chicago.)

Posed photographs were used by the city to promote the new subway via postcards, which touted improvements in ventilation, illumination, escalators, safety, and comfort. The August 1944 issue of *Architectural Forum* magazine opines, "America's newest underground shows a number of interesting improvements over previous jobs in spite of WPB [War Production Board] limitations." Chicago's subway also featured art moderne styling, fitting for the city that became the home of the New Bauhaus design school starting in 1937.

The Chicago Rapid Transit Company had a control room on the 12th floor of the Commonwealth Edison Building, where power could be turned on or off in sections of the new subway. The man on the right is a young George Krambles (1915–1999), just starting a career that eventually saw him serve as general manager of the Chicago Transit Authority. It was Krambles who flipped the switch turning on power in the State Street Subway when it opened on October 17, 1943. (J.J. Sedelmaier Collection.)

The State Street and Dearborn Subways featured continuous platforms throughout the downtown area. State's was the longer of the two, at 3,500 feet versus Dearborn's 2,500 feet. Continuous platforms gave the CRT (and later CTA) maximum flexibility. This may have been inspired by continuous platforms on some portions of the Loop "L", then in use. This postcard view may date to October 1943, as both tracks are shown in service. (J.J. Sedelmaier Collection.)

KEEP 'EM FLYING—
BUY WAR BONDS

EDWARD J. KELLY
MAYOR

CITY OF CHICAGO

OFFICE OF THE MAYOR

October 7, 1943

Mr. R. N. Wade
72 W. Adams Street
Chicago, Illinois

Dear Mr. Wade:

Construction and equipment of Chicago's first subway have now been completed. On Saturday, October 16, 1943, this new subway will be formally turned over to the Chicago Rapid Transit Company for immediate and permanent operation.

It is planned to commemorate this historical event with ceremonies appropriate to such an important contribution to the City's local transportation facilities. For this occasion, arrangements have been made for special elevated trains, operating from the North and from the South, to bring guests to the dedication that will occur within the tubes underneath Madison Street.

Mindful of your active interest in the progress and development of Chicago, I should like to have you join other civic, church, business, labor and professional leaders in these ceremonies, including a ride on the first trains.

You may board the special elevated train at the 58th Street "L" Station at exactly 10:10 A.M. This train will adhere rigidly to its scheduled time inasmuch as the regular elevated service cannot be disorganized.

The enclosed badge will admit you, without charge, to the Elevated Station platform.

Very truly yours,

Edward J Kelly

Mayor

In a letter to R.N. Wade, Mayor Edward J. Kelley invites him to attend opening ceremonies for the State Street Subway on October 16, 1943. At the event, Kelly said, "This is a proud day for Chicago—marking the celebration of an event which will go down in the city's history as probably the most significant evidence of its progress to date." (J.J. Sedelmaier Collection.)

The city's original State Street Subway plans called for the north subway portal to connect to the "L" at Chicago Avenue, where four elevated tracks were narrowed down to two. But as built, the subway connected to the "L" farther north at Willow Street to bypass a nearby triple curve that slowed down trains. The subway portal necessitated moving the "L" tracks outward, as shown in this 1943 photograph of the completed incline connection.

At midnight on October 16, 1943, a jubilant crowd of Chicagoans celebrate the long-awaited opening of Chicago's first subway at State and Madison Streets, the "world's busiest corner." The State Street Subway was 4.9 miles long and included nine new stations. The cost of this and the unfinished Dearborn-Milwaukee Subway was estimated at $57.2 million when first approved, and the federal government paid $25,967,000 of this. Ultimately, the cost came to $75 million. Chicago was the 18th city in the world to have a subway.

Beaming with civic pride, the Chicago family at left dressed up in their Sunday best for their first subway ride in October 1943. The descent of a train into the subway was as thrilling as a ride at Riverview amusement park. It is not surprising that the 1942 Steinmetz High School yearbook quotes Edmund R. Sadowski (1924–1996) saying he hoped to "live long enough to ride the Chicago Subway." The CRT ticket agent at right is at work in her booth on October 21, 1943. Agents made change and gave out transfers, while customers either deposited dimes into the nearby turnstile or showed the agent their transfers. Later, as fares increased, the Chicago Transit Authority sold tokens to be used in turnstiles.

On October 24, 1943, Secretary of the Interior Harold Ickes became a straphanger and went for a ride on the new State Street Subway. By then, the PWA had been reorganized into the Federal Works Administration (FWA), and Ickes was no longer in charge. Federal government grants for public transit were a thing of the past. Millions were serving in the armed forces, and the goal was to win the war. Nearly a quarter century would go by before Chicago received additional federal grants for mass transit construction.

Passengers are getting off a subway train of 4000-series rapid transit cars on October 21, 1943, a few days after the subway opened. Riders could get a free walking transfer, good for 15 minutes, allowing them to change trains with nearby elevated stations.

On October 18, 1943, a day after the State Street Subway opened, crowds of people wait on their trains at the platform. Notice how chaotic the real crowds look, with people going in all directions, compared with the earlier carefully posed photographs. (Photograph by George Kotalik.)

A woman pays her 10¢ fare at the mezzanine-level subway entrance at State and Monroe Streets on July 18, 1944. As originally built, the State Street Subway had underground walkways to several downtown retailers that were gradually expanded into a larger network called the Pedway. The Fair, shown here, was one of Chicago's earliest department stores. It was purchased by Montgomery Ward in 1957, and this location closed in 1984. (HB-08009-D, Chicago History Museum, Hedrich-Blessing Collection.)

The new subway entrances on State Street were functional but not flashy and included an air vent as part of their design. Many of the original kiosks are still in use 75 years later, usually with the addition of larger signage and some advertising, but this is how they looked in 1943.

Five

THE DEARBORN-
MILWAUKEE SUBWAY

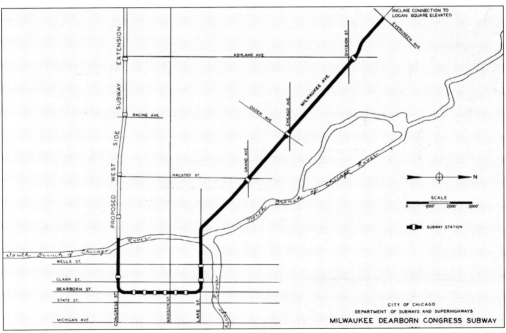

By 1951, when the Dearborn-Milwaukee Subway finally opened after years of delays, the tunnel was extended from Dearborn and Congress Streets to a point just west of the Chicago River. Until 1958, the LaSalle Street station was called Congress Terminal, and the subway tracks west of there were used for train storage. This map does show the planned extension into the median of the Congress Expressway, already under construction. (City of Chicago.)

Map of the Initial System of Subways

GENERAL PLAN
INITIAL SYSTEM OF SUBWAYS
CITY OF CHICAGO
DEPARTMENT OF SUBWAYS AND SUPERHIGHWAYS

The heavy black lines show the routes to be completed in 1941. Open lines indicate the stations while the dotted line marks the route of a future extension under Congress Street to Halsted Street.

—179

FIRST PUBLIC INSPECTION NEW CHICAGO SUBWAY

TOUR CONDUCTED UNDER AUSPICES
OF THE
WESTERN SOCIETY OF ENGINEERS

9 A. M. to 4 P. M. - March 30, 1940

CITY OF CHICAGO

EDWARD J. KELLY
Mayor

JAMES R. QUINN
Chairman, Committee on Local Transportation

P. W. A. PROJECT ILL. 1891-F

JOSHUA D'ESPOSITO
Project Engineer

DEPARTMENT OF SUBWAYS AND SUPERHIGHWAYS

RALPH H. BURKE
Chief Engineer

PHILIP HARRINGTON
Commissioner

On March 30, 1940, the Western Society of Engineers took a tour of one mile of completed subway tunnels on the northwest side. The owner of this brochure excitedly noted, "I was there!" The illustration on page 2 of this book appears to have been at least partly copied from the 1939 photograph shown here.

On June 6, 1940, a section of steel lining has been put in place for one of the Dearborn-Milwaukee Subway tubes under Dearborn Street near Lake Street, by the Harris and Selwyn Theaters. Cement was then poured over the steel, creating a tube wall 26½ inches thick. Tunneling in this area was done by the shield method of mining. The Harris and Selwyn building facades are now preserved as part of the Goodman Theatre complex. (City of Chicago.)

In May 1940, parts of the Dearborn-Milwaukee Subway are dug at the intersection of Milwaukee Avenue, Division Street, and Ashland Avenue. Eventually, a station was built at this location using the cut-and-cover technique. The eventual north subway portal was a short distance from here at Evergreen Avenue.

At left, Chicago's second subway makes a turn from Milwaukee Avenue onto Lake Street at the point shown here. By November 1940, the date of this picture, tunneling was about 80 percent complete for both subways. At right, on February 18, 1941, members of the State Street Council are shown riding a narrow-gauge train on an inspection tour of the Chicago subway. People attending early tours of the Dearborn-Milwaukee Subway likely rode this way too. (Left, City of Chicago.)

The completed subway bed at Division Street and Milwaukee Avenue was photographed on July 26, 1941. No tracks were yet in place, and none would be until the postwar era. (Peter Fish Studios for the City of Chicago.)

In 1942, tracks are being put back at Dearborn and Washington Streets by Chicago Surface Lines crane X-3 after construction of the Dearborn-Milwaukee Subway in this area. The subway was 80 percent finished when work stopped due to wartime material shortages and did not open until 1951.

There were many short, abandoned tunnels in downtown Chicago, some dating back to the 19th century. On September 22, 1947, a crane, after three tries, found the remains of an old, unused tunnel 200 feet long in the Chicago River near Congress Street. Workers sealed it off so it would not interfere with the Dearborn-Milwaukee Subway tunnel, then being built at this point.

New CTA rapid transit cars 6003 and 6004, signed for Logan Square, are shown pulling in to the old North Water Street stub-end terminal in 1950. After testing four experimental articulated trainsets (5001–5004), the CTA made some changes and improvements. Instead of an articulated car, the new models were permanently married pairs, which saved on the expense of control equipment. The Merchandise Mart, then owned by the Kennedy family, is at rear.

Charles R. Blade must have been a CRT and CTA favorite, as he was given the honor of piloting the first run of the new 6000-series cars shown here on August 16, 1950. By then, the 59-year-old Blade had been a motorman for 39 years. The test train is preparing to leave Logan Square terminal for its return trip downtown. Blade was also at the controls of the first official train on the State Street Subway in 1943. (Chicago Transit Authority.)

Guest Souvenir Permit

OFFICIAL OPENING
MILWAUKEE-DEARBORN-CONGRESS SUBWAY

WASHINGTON-MADISON STATION
11 a.m., Saturday, February 24, 1951

CITY OF CHICAGO
Martin H. Kennelly, Mayor

The city and CTA held opening ceremonies for the Dearborn-Milwaukee Subway on February 24, 1951, the day before regular service began. Former mayor Kelly had died the previous year. Harold Ickes would only live a short time himself, and it is not known if he ever rode this subway. Interestingly, Carter H. Harrison IV (1860–1953), who served as mayor for 12 years between 1897 and 1915, did live to see it. It is remarkable that one person's life could encompass so many events in the history of one city. (J.J. Sedelmaier Collection.)

This guest badge is from the opening ceremonies, which were held at 11:00 a.m. at the Dearborn and Madison subway station. Five special trains from different parts of the city brought 600 civic and community leaders to the event. The speakers included Mayor Martin Kennelly; Ralph Budd, chairman of the CTA; and Virgil E. Gunlock, commissioner of subways and superhighways. (J.J. Sedelmaier Collection.)

MILWAUKEE-DEARBORN
CONGRESS SUBWAY

OFFICIAL OPENING
February 24, 1951

Martin H. Kennelly, Mayor
City of Chicago

Above, Virgil E. Gunlock (1905–1963), head of the Chicago Department of Subways and Superhighways, addresses the crowd at the opening of the Dearborn-Milwaukee Subway on February 24, 1951. He later became chairman of the Chicago Transit Authority. Below, Mayor Kennelly addresses the same crowd. Both subway tubes were dedicated during mayoral campaigns, and both mayors (Kelly and Kennelly) were reelected. Kennelly, a successful businessman, was founder and first president of Allied Van Lines. He served as mayor from 1947 to 1955 but was considered too much a reformer by the regular Democrats, who refused to slate him for a third term in favor of Richard J. Daley (1902–1976).

The city issued a booklet extolling the virtues of its newest subway (right), this time with brand-new rapid transit cars. Mayor Kennelly wrote about the opening of the Milwaukee-Dearborn-Congress subway, stating that it was an "expression of the 'I WILL' spirit . . . which has made Chicago great." The February 1951 CTA *Transit News* also features a train of new 6000-series rapid transit cars emerging from the north portal of the Dearborn-Milwaukee Subway at Evergreen Avenue. The monthly employee magazine often went into greater detail about service changes and strategy than other publications.

the MILWAUKEE-
DEARBORN-CONGRESS
SUBWAY

Route No. 2 of Chicago's Initial System of Subways
FEBRUARY, 1951

CTA TRANSIT NEWS
FEBRUARY-1951

Mayor Kennelly cuts the ribbon for the Dearborn-Milwaukee Subway on February 24, 1951. Joining him are, from left to right, an unidentified CTA motorman (not Charles R. Blade); master of ceremonies Monte Blue; and Virgil E. Gunlock, head of the Chicago Department of Subways and Superhighways. Movie cowboy Blue (1887–1963) had a career going back to silent days. He even had a bit part in the infamous (and influential) 1915 D.W. Griffith film *The Birth of a Nation*. He was in town to work as emcee at the 13th annual Chicago Outdoors Show at Navy Pier, appearing alongside the Movieland Seals and Docky's Baseball Playing Dogs. (Chicago Transit Authority.)

Sometimes, when one door opens, another one closes. Humboldt Park "L" trains were planned to use the Dearborn-Milwaukee Subway in addition to Logan Square trains. But the Chicago Transit Authority decided to abandon the short branch, which ran parallel to nearby North Avenue. After neighborhood outcry, Humboldt Park got a brief reprieve, but service was ultimately abandoned on May 5, 1952. These passengers ride in one of the old wooden "L" cars on the last day of service.

Six

DISPLACED

When subway work started, Congress Street did not go west of State Street downtown. Ickes insisted that the city lengthen it, both as a route for extending the Dearborn-Milwaukee Subway and as part of the Congress Expressway. This extension had been a recommendation of the 1909 Burnham Plan. Building a subway underneath LaSalle Street station while maintaining regular train service proved to be especially difficult. Here is the state of construction as of March 11, 1949. The cleared area in the immediate foreground was once the location of the 13-story Monon Railroad Building.

In August 1938, CRT Metropolitan "L" car 2847 stops at Canal Street, where riders could change trains for Union Station. This westbound train was heading to both Logan Square and Humboldt Park. At the Damen and North station, it would be separated, with each car going a different way. The station remained in service until June 1958, when the Congress Street rapid transit line opened.

This aerial view of the old Main Post Office looks east and shows the area prior to construction of the Congress Expressway. Virtually all the buildings in a block-wide path in front of the Main Post Office had to be removed. The area in the middle of the building was set aside for highway use when it was built in 1933. After construction finished, the post office forgot about this and started using the space that eventually did become part of the highway. The city and post office had to negotiate a cost-sharing agreement to relocate the offending facilities.

The Peoria Street Bridge, shown under construction on October 25, 1950, was the very first span over the Congress Expressway. The bridges were built first, since it was easier to route traffic around them temporarily that way. Once a bridge was completed, the entire area nearby would be excavated.

Although hundreds of buildings were demolished for the new expressway, some were moved, including this five-story building, which is in transit from Congress and Peoria Streets to Harrison and Peoria Streets on September 2, 1949. The Garfield Park "L" is visible in the background.

CTA PCC streetcar 4061, a product of St. Louis Car Company, heads southbound on Route 8 at Halsted near Congress Street. A shoo-fly is under construction to divert streetcars around the site, where a bridge will soon be built for the Congress Expressway. The old Garfield Park "L" at rear remained in service until the new Congress Expressway median rapid transit line opened in June 1958. In this area, the "L" ran just north of the highway. This c. 1950 picture was taken looking north. Klein's Sporting Goods, at left, achieved notoriety because it sold Lee Harvey Oswald the mail-order rifle used to kill Pres. John F. Kennedy in 1963. (Photograph by Edward Frank Jr.)

On August 13, 1953, CTA trolley 630 headed north on Route 8, Halsted Street, via a new bridge over the Congress Expressway construction area. Robert Selle took this picture from the nearby Halsted Street "L" station seen in the previous picture. CTA Garfield Park trains began using temporary tracks west of here on Van Buren Street the following month. The Halsted station was not directly in the expressway footprint and remained in operation. Douglas Park trains, which also used this station, were not rerouted until 1954, when they were shifted to the Lake Street "L" via a new track connection.

Douglas Park trains were rerouted over the Lake Street "L" at Marshfield Junction in April 1954. A Douglas Park test train is at center, while the regular service train is on the old alignment. Moving Douglas Park service meant a nearly mile-long section of "L" could be torn down. The curved "L" track (left) is the original Douglas Park alignment. The truncated track in the center was last used in September 1953 by Garfield Park trains and CA&E interurbans. After Garfield Park trains were shifted to temporary grade-level tracks on Van Buren Street, nearly two miles of "L" to the west was demolished. A new north–south track connection was built to shift Douglas Park trains to the Lake Street "L". Today, this is the Paulina Connector, part of the Pink Line.

Chicago's "L"s were built by four separate companies. At Paulina and Lake Streets, two lines from different companies crossed. The upper section of track was last used in 1951 by Logan Square and Humboldt Park trains prior to the opening of the Dearborn-Milwaukee Subway. This 1953 image shows construction of a new connection, permitting Douglas Park trains to head downtown via the Lake Street "L". In 2006, the CTA renamed the Douglas Park "L" the Pink Line and rerouted it to use this track connection again, as it had from 1954 to 1958. (Chicago Transit Authority.)

On May 8, 1952, a two-car CTA Garfield Park "L" train stops at the Ogden Avenue station, followed by a three-car Chicago Aurora & Elgin interurban. Much of the area around the station has been cleared for the Congress Superhighway. (Photograph by Joe Kordick.)

This aerial view, looking east, shows the Garfield Park "L" and the future site of the Congress Superhighway as it appeared on September 2, 1950. Some demolition has already taken place. The highway follows the path of the "L" in the foreground, heading straight through the middle of the old Main Post Office in the background.

The former Western Avenue station on the Garfield Park "L" is being torn down in this 1954 view. Meanwhile, PCC streetcars head south on CTA Route 49, where they were replaced by buses in 1956. (Photograph by William C. Hoffman, Wien-Criss Archive.)

The "L" structure is being torn down near Ashland Avenue (1600 West) in 1954. By then, Douglas Park "L" service had been shifted to the Lake Street "L". A Garfield Park train can just barely be seen running on the Van Buren Street trackage at right. The tall building in the center, 333 South Ashland Avenue, is now called the Chicago & Midwest Regional Joint Board, Workers United Hall. It was designed by Walter Ahlschlager and opened in 1928. It became the most prominent building in an area known as "Union Row."

Until large-scale expressway demolitions began in 1949, some west side residents did not believe an expressway would ever be built. It had been talked about for many years, but little had been done other than land acquisition.

Chicago has a long tradition of moving entire buildings. Rather than tear down this west side two-flat apartment building, it was moved on May 21, 1954, from the north side of the 4900 block of Lexington Avenue to the south side, along with six others. The process involved rotating the buildings to face in the opposite direction. Today, this building can be found at 4927 Lexington Avenue, resting upon its second foundation. (Photograph by Frank Las.)

The Kilbourn Avenue station on the Garfield Park "L" had been closed and its stairways removed by the time this 1955 picture was taken. During the 1950s, the CTA closed several stations to speed up Garfield Park "L" service, due to the slow temporary section on Van Buren Street. This two-car train of CTA 4000s is about to cross the Congress Expressway construction site, but the highway does not appear to be open yet. The "L" tracks were higher than normal at this location to go over a nearby railroad.

The passing tracks indicate this picture was taken near the Gunderson Avenue station in Oak Park. The Forest Park gas holder tank, a local landmark for many years, is at rear, to the west. Then, as now, Gunderson Avenue is a side street in Oak Park, but it got its own "L" station in 1905, as this was a popular new subdivision. While the expressway was being built, CTA relocated this station to nearby Ridgeland Avenue but chose not to put a permanent station there. Neighborhood activists lobbied for secondary entrances to the Austin Boulevard and Oak Park Avenue stations, which serve much the same purpose.

For more than 50 years, the Garfield Park "L" crossed the Baltimore & Ohio Railroad at grade in Forest Park. This meant that "L" trains were often delayed by freight trains. In this mid-1950s view, a two-car CTA train of 6000-series "L" cars crosses the tracks. Note the Forest Park gas holder tank, mentioned on page 75. The view is to the northwest. With the construction of the Congress (now Eisenhower) Expressway, these tracks were grade-separated via a flyover.

This photograph shows an eastbound two-car Met "L" train at the old DesPlaines Avenue station, which was owned by the Chicago, Aurora & Elgin. The station was on the east side of the street, in an area now occupied by the Eisenhower Expressway. In the early 1950s, the CA&E began a piecemeal liquidation, selling off parts of its right-of-way. CTA, wanting to retain service to Forest Park, purchased CA&E's fixed assets between Laramie Avenue and DesPlaines Avenue for $1 million.

Seven

DEATH OF AN INTERURBAN

A westbound three-car CA&E train almost literally whistles past the graveyard before the Congress (now Eisenhower I-290) Expressway in this portion of Forest Park was constructed. The interurban ran just to the north of Harrison Street on an east–west alignment between two local cemeteries. This is right in the middle of the expressway today, and many graves had to be moved during construction.

From 1905 until 1953, the CA&E ran trains downtown over tracks of the Metropolitan West Side "L" to reach the Wells Street Terminal, shown in the foreground. Each of the four companies that built Chicago's elevated system had stub-end terminals just outside the Loop, but Wells, with four tracks, was the most extensive of these. The CTA stopped using this terminal in 1951, leaving the interurban as the only tenant. But with the 1953 service cutback, the terminal was surplus, and parts of it were demolished in 1955 to provide a new connection to the Loop for Garfield Park trains. By January 1960, when this picture was taken, no trains used these tracks. They were torn down in 1964.

On June 18, 1953, wooden CA&E car 28 heads up a westbound train at Canal Street. Nicknamed the "Sunset Lines," the CA&E was on the verge of heading off into the sunset, as it would voluntarily cut back service to Forest Park just three months later. (Photograph by Robert Selle.)

In this June 18, 1953 photograph, it is easy to see why the curve east of the Halsted Street "L" station was a photographer's favorite. A three-car "Roarin' Elgin" train, with wooden car 54 at the helm, heads west, while a CTA train of three wooden Met cars is close behind. Close to 50 years of precision timing and teamwork between the rapid transit companies and the CA&E (detailed in Bruce Moffat's fine book *Cooperation Moves the Public*) were about to come to an end. (Photograph by Robert Selle.)

No less than three Metropolitan "L" branches diverged at Marshfield Junction, seen here in 1952. Two Chicago, Aurora & Elgin interurbans pass, while two CTA trains are in the station. The building in the foreground will soon be torn down to make way for the expressway. This view looks east.

Taken from the same vantage point, these images detail the changes seen at the east end of the Western Avenue station within just a few years. Joe L. Diaz captured the 1940s image above, which shows a neighborhood full of tenements and businesses, likely overcrowded and suffering from overuse. Below, CA&E 458, a 1945 product of the St. Louis Car Company, heads a westbound three-car train at Western Avenue, around 1952 or 1953. The Van Buren Street temporary trackage is in place but has not been tested. Nearly every building in the picture above has been demolished. In the distance is the imposing structure of Richard T. Crane Medical Preparatory High School, otherwise known as Crane Tech. (Below, photograph by Robert Selle, Wien-Criss Archive.)

Loop-bound CA&E car 455 is preparing to stop at Kedzie Avenue on June 7, 1953. This station, unlike Western Avenue, was not in the expressway footprint, so the buildings surrounding it were not obliterated. CTA did not have to replace all the Garfield Park "L", only those portions that were in the highway's path. But over time, it became clear that there was an opportunity to provide a relatively low-cost, grade-separated right-of-way all the way to DesPlaines Avenue, and plans were changed. The ultimate cost of the new line came to $40 million. The Kedzie Avenue station remained in use by the CTA until June 1958. (Photograph by Robert Selle.)

Wooden CA&E car 46 is on the west end of an eastbound six-car train at Laramie Avenue. This picture was taken from a transfer bridge. The area to the right of the tracks is now occupied by the expressway. The "L" itself was not in the expressway footprint here. A few blocks to the east, there was a ramp leading up to the Cicero Avenue station, which was elevated. Until the early 1950s, the tracks between Laramie and DesPlaines Avenues were owned by the CA&E.

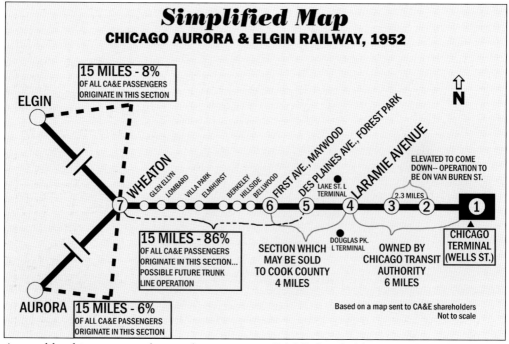

Simplified Map
CHICAGO AURORA & ELGIN RAILWAY, 1952

15 MILES - 8% OF ALL CA&E PASSENGERS ORIGINATE IN THIS SECTION

ELGIN

WHEATON

GLEN ELLYN LOMBARD VILLA PARK ELMHURST BERKELEY HILLSIDE BELLWOOD

FIRST AVE., MAYWOOD DES PLAINES AVE., FOREST PARK

LARAMIE AVENUE

LAKE ST. L TERMINAL

N

ELEVATED TO COME DOWN-- OPERATION TO BE ON VAN BUREN ST.

2.3 MILES

7 — 6 — 5 — 4 — 3 — 2 — **1**

15 MILES - 86% OF ALL CA&E PASSENGERS ORIGINATE IN THIS SECTION... POSSIBLE FUTURE TRUNK LINE OPERATION

DOUGLAS PK. L TERMINAL

SECTION WHICH MAY BE SOLD TO COOK COUNTY 4 MILES

OWNED BY CHICAGO TRANSIT AUTHORITY 6 MILES

CHICAGO TERMINAL (WELLS ST.)

AURORA **15 MILES - 6%** OF ALL CA&E PASSENGERS ORIGINATE IN THIS SECTION

Based on a map sent to CA&E shareholders
Not to scale

A map like this regenerated example went out to CA&E shareholders in 1952 explaining the railroad's position regarding expressway construction. It opposed the Van Buren Street operation as slow and unsafe. CA&E wanted to abandon all service west of Wheaton, just 14 percent of total ridership. East of Wheaton, it proposed temporarily replacing train service with buses, pending completion of the new CTA line. None of these plans came to pass. CA&E's management decided that its railroad was no longer viable and pursued a policy of liquidating assets and distributing the proceeds to shareholders. Continuing to provide a money-losing service for the indefinite future, in the absence of government subsidies, was not an option.

The Van Buren Street temporary trackage occupied the southern half of the street. Here, a CA&E train of steel cars is on the Garfield Park structure, within sight of the temporary tracks.

Riders experienced confusion and delays changing trains between the CA&E and CTA. Of all the joint timetables that were issued to commuters, this is the 14th and potentially the last. Between 1953 and 1957, the number of CA&E trains dwindled, as the interurban lost about half of its ridership.

A two-car CA&E train pulls up to a platform at the DesPlaines Avenue terminal, where Chicago Transit Authority passengers could transfer for trains headed west between 1953 and 1957. Financial losses were estimated at $3.3 million.

SUNDAYS

WESTBOUND			EASTBOUND		
At Quincy Station CTA Leave	Desplaines Ave. at Forest Park CTA Arrive	CA&E Leave	Desplaines Ave. at Forest Park CA&E Arrive	CTA Leave	At La Salle Station CTA Arrive
AM	AM	AM	AM	AM	AM
12:00	12:30	*12:35	12:53	1:01	1:31
12:50	1:20	1:25	**1:17	1:26	1:56
1:40	2:10	2:20	3:12	3:26	3:56
2:35	3:05	3:25	6:00	6:01	6:32
6:09	6:39	*6:55	7:13	7:16	7:47
6:56	7:26	7:40	**7:52	7:54	8:24
7:41	8:11	*8:25	8:48	8:54	9:25
8:34	9:04	9:10	**9:22	9:30	10:01
9:22	9:52	*9:55	10:13	10:16	10:49
9:58	10:28	10:35	**10:52	10:55	11:27
10:46	11:16	*11:25	11:48	11:53	12:25
11:36	12:08	12:10	**12:22	12:31	1:04
12:15	12:46	*12:55	1:13	1:20	1:52
1:03	1:35	1:40	**1:52	1:58	2:31
1:52	2:23	*2:25	2:48	2:56	3:29
2:30	3:02	3:10	**3:22	3:25	3:58
3:19	3:50	*4:00	4:13	4:14	4:46
4:17	4:48	4:55	**4:52	4:52	5:25
4:55	5:27	*5:30	5:48	5:50	6:23
5:34	6:05	6:10	**6:36	6:41	7:12
6:22	6:54	*6:55	7:13	7:22	7:53
7:11	7:42	*7:50	**7:52	7:53	8:24
8:02	8:33	8:35	8:28	8:35	9:06
8:44	9:15	*9:25	**8:57	9:06	9:37
9:35	10:06	10:10	**10:07	10:07	10:38
10:17	10:48	*10:55	10:48	10:49	11:20
11:08	11:39	11:45	**11:47	11:50	12:21

A.M. Time in Light Figures.
P.M. Time in Dark Figures.

*WESTBOUND—These trains serve Aurora, Batavia, Geneva, St. Charles, Elgin and other points west of Wheaton. Consult your CA&E timecard for further information.

**EASTBOUND—This service leaves from Aurora, Batavia, Geneva, St. Charles, Elgin and serves points west of Wheaton. Consult your CA&E timecard for further information.

All CA&E trains serve Wheaton.

Schedules subject to change without notice.

TIMETABLE for CHICAGO, AURORA and ELGIN RY. PASSENGERS

Listed on the following pages are the schedules of CTA (Garfield Park) and CA&E trains that make connections at the joint terminal of the two services at Desplaines Avenue, Forest Park.

For the convenience of CA&E passengers, this schedule information shows the following:

1. Leaving time of westbound CTA trains at Quincy and Wells downtown loop station, arrival of these trains at the CTA-CA&E joint terminal at Desplaines Avenue, Forest Park, and the departure times of westbound CA&E trains with which connections are made at that point.

2. Arrival time of CA&E trains at the Desplaines Avenue, Forest Park, terminal, the departure times of eastbound CTA trains with which connections are made, and arrival time of CTA trains at La Salle Street station in the loop.

Among the stations served by CTA trains (westbound and eastbound) are Canal, Kedzie, Cicero, Laramie and Oak Park where passengers formerly boarded and alighted from CA&E trains.

EFFECTIVE MAY 19, 1957

ISSUED JOINTLY
BY
CHICAGO TRANSIT AUTHORITY
AND
CHICAGO, AURORA AND ELGIN RY.

(Timetable No. 14)

CA&E owned land crossing the DesPlaines River, which Cook County desperately needed to bridge a gap between two highways. Negotiations over its sale began in 1945 and dragged on for 12 years. County officials felt CA&E wanted too much money. Whether a quid pro quo was reached cannot be proven, but local courts allowed CA&E to temporarily abandon passenger service on July 3, 1957; and on July 31, CA&E agreed to sell this property for $1.2 million. By 1959, CA&E's bridge and tracks were relocated north of the new highway, but no trains ever ran on them. Cars 401 and 431 are shown heading west in 1953. (Photograph by Robert Selle.)

Even after the July 3, 1957, abandonment of passenger service, there were efforts to bring CA&E back. On March 6, 1958, a CA&E train was chartered and dubbed the "Mass Transit Special." It carried officials who sought to resume service and made stops at several suburbs served by the CA&E. Crowds turned out to greet them, including at least one marching band. Here, the train is at York Road in Elmhurst. Unfortunately, efforts to subsidize CA&E by taxing suburbanites failed. CA&E operated freight service until 1959, when this too was finally abandoned and the railroad dismantled. (Photograph by Robert W. Gibson.)

Eight

THE LAST STREET RAILWAY

On August 29, 1953, a three-car Garfield Park "L" test train is westbound on Van Buren Street at about Western Avenue. The photographer was riding a regular westbound train on the "L" nearby. (Photograph by Robert Selle.)

Wooden piles are being driven into the earth on September 4, 1951, the beginnings of a ramp at Aberdeen Street that would bring Garfield Park "L" trains down to the surface to run for nearly 2.5 miles in the south half of Van Buren Street. Originally, trolley poles were to be added to trains, but there were material shortages due to the Korean War. Ultimately, third rail was used instead, and the train tracks were fenced off as much as possible.

In the photograph above, taken by Raymond DeGroote Jr., two CTA Met cars ascend the ramp connecting the temporary Van Buren route with the existing "L" near Aberdeen Street. "L" car 2858 was built by Pullman in 1906. Wooden "L" cars were being phased out by the CTA as fast as possible. By the time of their retirement, some cars were more than 50 years old. Below is a view of much the same scene but taken looking to the west, the opposite direction. A Douglas Park train is on the old four-track structure, indicating that this picture was taken in either late 1953 or early 1954. The Racine Avenue station and Throop Street Shops are in the background. Temporarily used for parking, the surrounding area has already been cleared in preparation for the Congress Expressway.

A two-car (2807 and 2704) CTA test train crosses Western Avenue on Van Buren Street heading east on August 19, 1953. These trains, with reflective strips on their sides, were used to familiarize motorists with the street-level operation, which began service on September 20. The Garfield Park "L" station at Western Avenue, in the background, closed when the temporary route opened. (Photograph by Robert Selle.)

A Garfield Park train is headed east on Van Buren Street in late 1953 or early 1954. The view was captured from above, standing on the old "L" platform at Marshfield Junction, which was still being used for Douglas Park "L" trains. The streetcar tracks visible on Paulina Street were used by Ashland Avenue streetcars, which were replaced by buses on February 13, 1954.

This eastbound 4000-series train, headed by 4446, is on Van Buren Street at Paulina Street on April 21, 1957. The new 1954 structure for Douglas trains is behind the facing train. Paulina's streetcar tracks, last used in early 1954 for Ashland Avenue streetcars, are no longer evident. (Photograph by Raymond DeGroote Jr.)

A Douglas Park train crosses over the Van Buren right-of-way near Paulina Street (1700 West), while a Garfield Park train heads west below. This may be 1954, as the old "L" structure is still in place east of here. It could not be torn down until Douglas Park trains were rerouted via new connections to the Lake Street "L", about one mile north on the Paulina Connector. Notice how one of the Garfield tracks takes a dogleg around the "L" supports.

Taken on December 11, 1955, this photograph captures two Garfield Park 4000-series "Baldies" (4248 and 4247) on the Van Buren Street trackage as seen from a passing Douglas Park train traversing the new structure built to connect Douglas Park trains to the Lake Street "L". The completed bridge over the highway is a part of Ogden Avenue. (Photograph by Raymond DeGroote Jr.)

CTA PCC streetcar 7037 meets CTA Baldie "L" car 4225 at Western Avenue and Van Buren Street in September 1955. The streetcar (left) was built around 1948 by the St. Louis Car Company, while the "L" car (right) was a 1915 product of the Cincinnati Car Company. (Photograph by Thomas H. Desnoyers.)

A Green Hornet "L" car (left) meets a Green Hornet streetcar (right) at Western Avenue and Van Buren Street on June 16, 1954. The earliest rapid transit 6000s featured flat doors and double headlights. These specimens are seen heading eastbound on Van Buren Street. The postwar St. Louis PCC streetcar 4273 is northbound on the Western Avenue shoo-fly, which was constructed for use while the bridge over the Congress Expressway was being built. The original streetcar tracks are seen in the foreground. (Photograph by William C. Hoffman, Wien-Criss Archive.)

The Van Buren Street trackage at Rockwell Street (2600 West Van Buren Street) was lowered, creating an underpass to clear the Chicago & North Western and Pennsylvania Railroad tracks above. Here, CTA tracks are in the middle, instead of simply taking up the south half of the street. The train is heading west.

CTA 2730 is westbound at Van Buren Street and Ashland Avenue, on the reroute of the Garfield Park "L", around 1954. A sign hanging on the front of the car indicates this train connects with a CA&E train leaving DesPlaines Avenue at 6:12 p.m. Streetcars last ran on Ashland Avenue in early 1954, and the tracks have already been removed at this location.

A two-car CTA train 6041-6042 is westbound at Western Avenue on the Van Buren Street temporary trackage in this photograph, taken on February 22, 1955. Rerouting caused by Congress Expressway construction had a lot to do with the demise of the CA&E. Not only did construction slow service down to a crawl, but the interurban considered the operation potentially unsafe.

A two-car train of CTA 4000s runs along the temporary Van Buren Street trackage around 1954 or 1955. Although temporary in nature, the Van Buren Street right-of-way was built to a high-quality standard. There were no crossing gates, and trains came to a complete stop at all intersections before carefully proceeding across.

A three-car CTA train descends the ramp connecting the temporary trackage on Van Buren Street with the existing Garfield Park "L" at Sacramento Boulevard. This was one of two places (the other being near Kostner Avenue) where the Garfield Park "L" crossed the expressway footprint.

A three-car train of wooden Met cars is headed east on the old "L" structure with the new temporary alignment in the background. The "L" had many curves, as the private companies that built the rails sometimes had difficulty buying all the properties necessary to put them in a straight line. Rather than pay exorbitant prices, they would simply reroute their lines.

On September 20, 1953, a three-car wooden test train is on the Sacramento Boulevard connecting ramp about to descend to ground level. The origin of the middle, open-platform car is unknown; however, similar cars were used on the Ravenswood line, so it is not unlikely that it was borrowed for this test. This picture was taken right when service was set to begin on the new ground-level Van Buren Street trackage. (Photograph by Raymond DeGroote Jr.)

A two-car "L" train goes down the ramp to the Van Buren Street trackage at California Avenue. The new CTA station in the expressway median is a strong indication this picture was taken in 1958, just before the Congress Street line was put into service.

An eastbound two-car train is stopped at Ogden Avenue and Van Buren Street. The nearby Damen-Ogden-Paulina CTA station appears finished, suggesting the photograph was likely taken in 1958. Today, this station, renamed for the nearby Illinois Medical District, is being modernized.

Nine

SUBWAYS AND SUPERHIGHWAYS

The Congress Street Expressway ends downtown, and this is how the east end appeared in 1956. Much thought was given to dispersing downtown auto traffic. Ramps at left and right connect to the then-new lower level of Wacker Drive. The open area surrounding the highway was originally planned to have an underground turning loop for the Dearborn-Milwaukee Subway, which terminated nearby at LaSalle Street from 1951 to 1958. Around 1948, it was decided this would be too expensive, so the subway used a stub-end terminal with a crossover track for those seven years. The LaSalle Street station was then called Congress Street Terminal.

By May 18, 1954, work was far along on the expressway east of Halsted Street (800 West). There are four subway portals, although only two were used when the West Side Subway opened in 1958. The original plan from 1946 called for Lake Street "L" trains to be routed into the Congress Expressway median near Kedzie Avenue via a new subway. The plan was to have four tracks in the Congress Expressway from Kedzie Avenue to Halsted Street, where Lake Street trains were to go into a Clinton Street Subway. In combination with the tubes on Lake Street, Dearborn Street, and the Congress Expressway, this would have formed a subway loop. By the early 1950s, these plans were scrapped, and a decision was made to replace the entire Garfield Park "L". Extra space remains in the Congress Expressway median for tracks that were never built. (Photograph by Bob Kotalik.)

What appears to be a large ditch is actually the Congress Expressway under construction around 1954. This image captures the view looking east from about Ashland Avenue (1600 West). The temporary CTA trackage on Van Buren Street is at the left. The bridge is a part of Loomis Street (1400 West).

In a general view of construction at Congress Street and Pulaski Road on July 28, 1955, Mayor Richard J. Daley swings a hammer to drive the first spike into the rail. This was the beginning of track construction in the median and preceded the opening of this portion of highway by several months. The section near Pulaski Road was a convenient place to begin, as it was near ground level and not depressed in a cut, as is most of the highway. (Photograph by Ralph Arvidson.)

Mayor Richard J. Daley drives the first rail spike for the Congress Expressway median line at Pulaski Road on July 8, 1955. It would take nearly three more years to finish the Congress Expressway line. (Photograph by Ralph Arvidson.)

On February 9, 1956, workmen brave the cold weather to lay tracks for the Congress Expressway median line at about 900 West. Rails were fastened down with brackets and spikes. (Photograph by Larry Nocerino.)

On October 8, 1955, this was the view looking east from Kostner Avenue (4400 West). Note the minimal fencing separating tracks from the highway. A Kostner CTA station opened in 1962 as the result of lobbying by three local aldermen whose wards were nearby. It closed in 1973.

The Congress Expressway is pictured partially open around 1956–1957. Tracks are in the median, but no third rail or stations yet. Meanwhile, the old Garfield Park alignment is still in place, including the double-island Halsted Street "L" station, although two of the four original tracks have been removed.

The Garfield Park "L" crossed the Congress Expressway at about Sacramento Boulevard (3000 West). At left, just north of the highway, was a ramp that brought trains down to ground level and the temporary Van Buren Street alignment. This picture probably dates to 1956, as this portion of highway is now open, but wooden cars are still being used on the "L".

A two-car train of CTA 4000s crosses the Congress (now Eisenhower) Expressway at Kostner Avenue (4400 West) in August 1956. Here, the old "L" structure is supported from beneath.

Virgil Gunlock, CTA chairman of the board, looks at 12 feet of water in the subway at the LaSalle and Congress station on July 13, 1957. There had been a downpour, and since the expressway cut was not yet landscaped, mud flowed into the pumps that were meant to keep the roadway dry, clogging them. Rainwater found a convenient drain in the new subway tube. The CTA managed to pump out the flooded tunnel the following day.

Dennis Headley, a CTA ticket agent, points to the flooded subway at the LaSalle and Congress station on July 13, 1957. The water level has gone all the way to the stairs at the subway entrance. It was pumped out by the following day.

Workmen William Metzger (left) and Dennis Moriarty wash the muck left on the platform by the flood where water entered the subway at Congress and LaSalle Streets on July 14, 1957. The subways were once again flooded in April 1992 due to their proximity to the Chicago freight tunnels, which were breached.

By September 1957, when this picture was taken, the Congress Expressway was already open as far west as Laramie Avenue (5200 West), but construction had not yet reached suburban Oak Park. The situation was complicated by the need to move both the CTA tracks and those of the Baltimore & Ohio Chicago Terminal (B&OCT), a freight line. First, the existing CTA tracks (center) were moved to the north (right), and new temporary stations such as this one at Oak Park Avenue were built. Next, the B&OCT tracks (left) were moved north, using the former CTA tracks. Then, a trench was dug at left for the permanent location of both sets of tracks. Once the tracks were moved, the rest of the area could be dug out and the roadway built.

On July 1, 1957, ironworkers Boller Boll (left) and Bill Magorn work on the aluminum support columns for the station at Keeler Avenue. (Photograph by Bill Knefel.)

Workers Dale Mueller (left) and Tom Shue install fiberglass panels in a Congress line ramp leading to a station entrance on December 9, 1957. The full-length fiberglass panels on these station ramps soon became a problem, as they shielded would-be robbers from view. Eventually, they were partially removed. (Photograph by Bill Knefel.)

On April 7, 1958, with the opening of the West Side Subway about two months away, workers are finishing construction of the ramp that will take Douglas Park trains into the Congress Expressway median. Today, CTA Pink Line trains, which replaced the Douglas Park line, continue to the left and run downtown over the Lake Street/Green Line route via the Paulina Connector. Note the CTA train of 6000s, running on the temporary Van Buren Street trackage.

In this March 17, 1958, photograph by Kelly Powell, construction is going on related to the Northwest Expressway. By 1958, any such work for the Congress Expressway had been taken care of years earlier. At this time, CTA service was still running on the old Met "L" east of Aberdeen Street (1100 West) and crossed the Northwest Expressway footprint just east of Halsted Street (800 West). Once service in this area was shifted to the new expressway median line in June 1958, this section of "L" was removed.

The Northwest (now Kennedy) Expressway is under construction in 1958, and the view is looking south from Madison Street. In the background, trains are still running on the old Garfield Park "L", which crosses the highway going east to west. As the previous picture shows, the "L" was shored up to allow expressway excavation around it. Once the new Congress line opened on June 22, the structure was removed. The Northwest Expressway opened on November 5, 1960, three days before the presidential election.

On June 10, 1958, workers put the finishing touches on the Congress Expressway interchange at Halsted Street. There are four subway portals at this location, although only two were ever used. The unused portals were intended for the Clinton Street Subway, which was never built. This would have created a complete downtown subway loop. The city's original plans were to reroute the Lake Street "L" into the Congress line and then into this Clinton Street Subway so that trains could go around this subway loop and allow parts of the Loop "L" to be torn down.

The new entrance to the Congress line station at Damen Avenue is typical of all that were put into service in 1958. It is a concrete building measuring 42 feet by 21 feet. The interiors featured glazed tile and fluorescent lighting. When the Kostner Avenue station was opened in 1962, it was given a somewhat smaller entrance, as the CTA did not expect it to have many riders. (Chicago Transit Authority.)

A CTA test train is on the new Congress Expressway median line in 1958, while a regular Garfield Park train is on the old structure about to descend to the Van Buren Street trackage. In the background, the Morgan Street entrance to the new Halsted Street (800 West) station is visible.

CTA chairman Virgil Gunlock and Julia Riordan, who worked in the CTA's public information department, inspect posters at Keeler Avenue announcing the impending opening of the West Side Subway in June 1958. A dedication ceremony with Mayor Richard J. Daley officiating was held on June 20, and free rides were given the following day. An estimated 20,000 people rode the new line then, which perhaps not coincidentally was the day the last Chicago streetcar ran. CTA chose a day when this event would receive less press attention.

Dedication ceremonies for the new West Side Subway (later called the Congress rapid transit line) were held at the Morgan Street overpass on June 20, 1958. That same day, a CTA test train heads west from Morgan Street, while regular service continues nearby on the old Garfield Park "L" structure. The following day, the CTA offered free rides on the new line as far west as Cicero Avenue (4800 West). Regular Congress line service began on June 22.

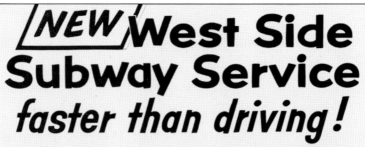

/NEW/ West Side Subway Service
faster than driving!

Only 12 minutes from Pulaski Road...17 minutes from Oak Park...23 minutes from Forest Park ...*a saving of up to 30%!*

Fast, safe, comfortable all-metal cars are assigned to this new service. Train operation is to be safeguarded by the latest type block signal and automatic train brake trip system. Twenty-seven hazardous street crossings are being eliminated. Through service is now provided between the West and Northwest sections of Chicago by way of the Central Business District.

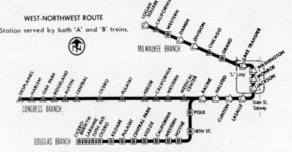

WEST-NORTHWEST ROUTE

△ Station served by both 'A' and 'B' trains.

COMPARE THESE RUNNING TIMES
WITH THE TIME IT TAKES TO DRIVE AND PARK

There are fourteen stations along the new subway—ten in Chicago, two in Oak Park, and two in Forest Park.

CHICAGO STATIONS	SUBURBAN STATIONS
Clinton and Congress....1 Min. to Loop	Austin Boulevard, Oak Park...............17 Mins. to Loop
*Halsted and Congress...3 Mins. to Loop	Ridgeland Avenue, Oak Park (temporary)....19 " " "
*Racine and Congress....4 " " "	Oak Park Avenue, Oak Park...............20 " " "
*Medical Center (Ogden-Paulina-Damen). 5 " " "	Harlem Avenue, Forest Park..............21 " " "
Western and Congress...7 " " "	Desplaines Avenue, Forest Park..............23 Mins. to Loop
California and Congress. 9 " " "	
*Kedzie and Congress...10 " " "	*Denotes station with auxiliary en-
*Pulaski and Congress..12 " " "	trance-exit facilities: At Morgan, Loomis,
*Cicero and Congress...14 " " "	Paulina, Damen, Homan, Keeler and
Central and Congress..16 Mins. to Loop	Lavergne.

Ride the new subway! It's the fastest way to go—
No street traffic delay, and no traffic woe!

CHICAGO TRANSIT AUTHORITY

The CTA was justifiably proud of its new, faster service, which reduced travel times between Cicero Avenue and downtown by 30 percent. When the Congress line opened in 1958, the new alignment only went as far as Lotus Avenue (5432 West). The remaining section of the Garfield Park "L" to the west ran at ground level, and construction of the Congress Expressway was in process.

By February 8, 1958, when this picture was taken by John McCarthy, Congress Expressway construction had reached 5800 West, between Central Avenue and Austin Boulevard on Chicago's far west side. A small portion of the south end of Columbus Park was shaved off for the highway footprint. A two-car CTA Garfield Park train heads west on temporary trackage at the north end of the construction site, and this view looks northeast. (Chicago History Museum, ICHi-065871.)

In 1959, a woman working in a nearby office observes expressway construction at Oak Park Avenue. Both the Baltimore & Ohio freight line and the CTA rapid transit line are still running on the surface in a temporary alignment at the north end of the highway footprint. Once the tracks were moved into their permanent layout, expressway lanes could be built.

Work is under way at the DesPlaines Avenue terminal to both reconfigure the terminal and build the adjacent Congress Expressway. This photograph was taken looking east on April 4, 1959.

This photograph, taken between March and July 1960, shows the temporary Harlem Avenue station on today's CTA Blue Line in suburban Oak Park during construction of what is now I-290. These are the permanent tracks, still in use today, but the new Harlem Avenue station was still under construction. The view looks east. The single-car units making up the two-car train on the right were first put in service in 1959 and have provision for trolley poles. These were intended for use on the CTA's Evanston branch. The temporary station was built on top of a crossover track.

On October 12, 1960, Illinois governor William Stratton cuts the ribbon celebrating the opening of the last section of the Congress Expressway, while Cook County Board president Daniel Ryan Jr. (left) and Mayor Richard J. Daley (right) look on.

The last section of the Congress Expressway formally opened on October 12, 1960. A marching band is on hand for the formal dedication ceremonies in suburban Oak Park. The highway opened in stages between Chicago and Maywood, going to Laramie Avenue in late 1955, then Central Avenue early in 1960. The section opened here went from Central Avenue to First Avenue in Maywood. (Photograph by Joseph Zack.)

The Congress Expressway had just opened in October 1960 when this picture was taken looking east at Oak Park Avenue (6800 West). Only two lanes of traffic are in use eastbound at this point, and the new Oak Park Avenue CTA station can be seen in the background.

The Congress Expressway opened on October 12, 1960, through Oak Park. The village only allowed three lanes of traffic in each direction, which caused immediate traffic jams that have persisted to this day. The areas on the side of the roadway have not yet been landscaped, and the median section in this location was left empty after Oak Park refused to allow an additional ramp at East Avenue. This section of highway was the last link connecting Central Avenue and First Avenue. (Photograph by Bob Kotalik.)

The CTA "Morgan middle" crossover track (between Racine Avenue and Morgan Street), seen here in 1961, allows the short-turning of trains. By then, the old "L" structure was completely removed and the expressway landscaped.

The Kostner Avenue station (4400 West) on the Congress line was unique in that it opened more than four years after the others. The city and CTA did not want to build a station at this location, on a curved section of track, but neighborhood pressure led the city council to approve an ordinance for it in 1955. Planners anticipated low ridership, but after legal action was threatened, construction started shortly before this picture was taken on August 29, 1961. The station, which opened on August 5, 1962, never attracted many riders and was closed in 1973.

By the time this picture was taken, on December 27, 1963, the Garfield Park "L" was but a memory. An eastbound Congress Expressway "A" train, consisting of later 6000-series cars with curved doors, heads west near Cicero Avenue, with the Belt Railway overpass in the background.

Ten

SUBWAYS SINCE 1960

When this picture was taken in the late 1960s, the Logan Square terminal at 2523 North Kedzie Boulevard was as far as any CTA train would travel into the northwest side of the city. By 1984, this route (now called the Blue Line) was extended 12 miles to O'Hare Airport. (Chicago Transit Authority.)

Construction of the mile-long Milwaukee-Kimball Subway, which opened on February 1, 1970, is visible in this aerial view of Logan Square. The tall object is the Illinois Centennial Memorial Column, built in 1918 to celebrate the 100th anniversary of Illinois's statehood. The subway provided a rapid transit connection to the new median line along the nearby Kennedy Expressway. The city's original plans called for a connection in an open cut farther east of Logan Square. Local activists lobbied for a subway extension along Milwaukee Avenue instead.

Unlike the Initial System of Subways, which were largely dug by tunneling using a shield, the Milwaukee-Kimball Subway was built using the cut-and-cover method, which produces square tunnels instead of round. Here, the photographer is looking north along Kimball Avenue from Milwaukee Avenue around 1968 or 1969. (Photograph by Raymond DeGroote Jr.)

Riders are shown disembarking at the new Belmont Avenue subway station in April 1970 on what is now the O'Hare branch of the CTA Blue Line. Stations along this section were designed by the firm Skidmore, Owings, & Merrill, famous for International Style architecture. Service in 1970 was extended from Logan Square to Jefferson Park and in 1984 to O'Hare Airport. The train at left is made up of 2200-series "L" cars, built by the Budd Company, which were put into service along with the new Kennedy and Dan Ryan lines. (Chicago Transit Authority.)

After 44 years of service, the CTA's 2200-series rapid transit cars were retired on August 8, 2013, with this last run. This picture was taken at Sayre Avenue on a section of the Kennedy Expressway median line that first opened in 1984. The nearby Harlem Avenue station is in the distance, and the view looks west.

CTA "L" cars 6141 and 6142 pause briefly in the State Street Subway while waiting for a train to move ahead on a May 29, 1988, fantrip. The 6000-series cars were ordered by the CTA to provide service on the Dearborn-Milwaukee Subway, which first opened in 1951. They ran in service for 40 years and came to symbolize the CTA during this era. In 2017, two pairs of 6000s returned to CTA property for the first time in decades and will eventually be restored as part of the CTA's historical fleet, used for charters and special events.

One of the original 1943 ticket booths from the State Street Subway was used for 67 years and appears here shortly before it was removed from the North and Clybourn station in 2010. The CTA has since transitioned to an all-electronic fare payment system called Ventra. Booths are occupied by customer service assistants instead of ticket-takers. (Photograph by Kevin Zolkiewicz.)

Some of the original signage is still in place, embedded in subway tile at the Milwaukee and Division station, as seen in this 2014 photograph. A variation of the Futura typeface was used to provide riders with clear, concise, and unadorned information. Easy-to-clean subway tile is being used in more and more places today, including many kitchens.

More original signage from the Milwaukee and Division station was still in place in 2014. When the Initial System of Subways opened, they were a triumph of Art Moderne styling. Over time, much of this stylistic unity has been lost or obscured, leading city planner Dennis McClendon to quip that the original stations need "remodeling, not remuddling."

Extensive modifications have been made at some subway stations, as seen in this view of the State and Jackson station in 2018. Mosaic tiles are installed in the ceiling with designs reminiscent of some New York City subways. Elevators are now retrofitted into stations to make public transportation more accessible, and lighting has been improved. Other amenities, like cell phone service, have been added for public convenience.

Even in 2018, some subway platforms, like the North and Clybourn station, have hardly changed from their original appearance, save for the addition of larger signs using the CTA's preferred Helvetica typeface. Subway enthusiasts are eager to pay tribute to the design of the Initial System of Subways and envision a retro subway station in the same nostalgic fashion employed at the Quincy and Wells station on the Loop "L".

The North and Clybourn station, the only one aboveground on the Initial System of Subways, was renovated in 2010 thanks to funding from Apple. The former bus turnaround in front of the rear-facing, wedge-shaped station was turned into a pedestrian plaza that connects to an adjacent Apple Store. Little change was made to the station interior.

Chicago's subways feature a continuous walkway for rider and employee safety. This photograph was taken at the north end of the Milwaukee and Division stop. This track was built using the cut-and-cover technique, hence the square shape of the tube at this location. There were also signaling improvements. Much of the "L" depended upon "on sight" operation, with short headways and large numbers of trains. The subway had a modern signal system, which kept an open block of space between trains. If a train ran through a red signal, brakes were automatically applied. This was a significant improvement in safety and paved the way for the introduction of cab signals in the 1960s.

Over time, fewer and fewer original subway kiosks remain, replaced by newer versions in a variety of unrelated styles, some looking futuristic, others reminiscent of styles that predate the subway itself. This entrance to the Dearborn and Jackson station is on the west side of the street in front of the landmark Monadnock Building, the north half of which at 215 feet is the tallest ever built using load-bearing brick.

An original hanging subway sign was still in use at the LaSalle and Congress station in 2018. Some of the original 1943 subway signage was made of Masonite instead of metal due to wartime material shortages.

This c. 1950 ticket booth, now used by CTA customer assistants, was still in place at the LaSalle and Congress station in 2018. While very similar in appearance to the ticket booths in the State Street Subway, some decorative elements (such as floor and wall coverings) in the Dearborn-Milwaukee Subway were made of lesser quality as a means of saving money. In 1950, the city had to float a $2 million bond issue to complete the subway.

When subway stations opened, pay phones were among the amenities. Since pay phones have become obsolete due to widespread cell phone usage, the CTA has blocked off this area at the LaSalle and Congress station and uses the space to display vintage photographs. On the left are examples of 1950s subway advertisements, and on the right is a 1950s photograph captured as this CTA conductor waits for the doors to close before his train can proceed northbound to Logan Square. Notice that the conductor is riding between cars, a dangerous practice that was soon eliminated.

Passengers at the O'Hare station exit the train and head for the stairs and escalators in this 2018 photograph. In the early hours of March 4, 2014, a four-car CTA train failed to stop before hitting the bumper post at the end of the line and went partway up the stairs, injuring 34 people and causing over $11 million in damage. An investigation by the National Transportation Safety Board determined that the train operator, who was later fired, had fallen asleep. As a result, the station was closed for nearly a week. The speed limit in the station terminal area was also reduced from 25 to 15 miles per hour.

The O'Hare station was designed by the firm of Murphy/Jahn. Architect Helmut Jahn (born in 1940) took control of C.F. Murphy Associates in 1981 with the retirement of Charles F. Murphy (1890–1985). Murphy began his career in 1911, when he became a secretary at the offices of Daniel H. Burnham and Company. In the late 1930s, his firm, Shaw, Naess & Murphy, designed the North and Clybourn station building. His career provided a living link between pioneer planner Burnham, the International Style of the 1930s, and the postmodernism of a later era.

A CTA Red Line train emerges from the south portal of the State Street Subway on July 12, 2013. These trains normally use the nearby Howard–Dan Ryan subway connector, but when this picture was taken, the Dan Ryan rapid transit line was being rebuilt. After 75 years, Chicago's Initial System of Subways serves as the backbone of the city's rapid transit system and will continue to do so for a long time to come.

Discover Thousands of Local History Books
Featuring Millions of Vintage Images

Arcadia Publishing, the leading local history publisher in the United States, is committed to making history accessible and meaningful through publishing books that celebrate and preserve the heritage of America's people and places.

Find more books like this at
www.arcadiapublishing.com

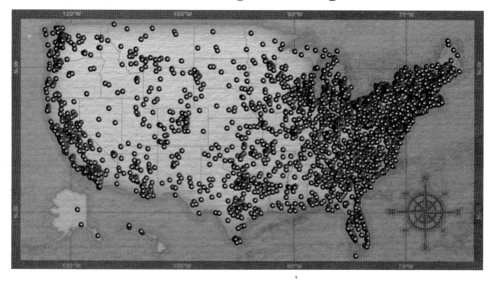

Search for your hometown history, your old
stomping grounds, and even your favorite sports team.

Consistent with our mission to preserve history on a local level, this book was printed in South Carolina on American-made paper and manufactured entirely in the United States. Products carrying the accredited Forest Stewardship Council (FSC) label are printed on 100 percent FSC-certified paper.

MADE IN THE
USA